SHEPHERD'S NOTES

Shepherd's Notes Titles Available

SHEPHERD'S NOTES COMMENTARY SERIES

Old Testament

9-780-805-490-282 Genesis
9-780-805-490-565 Exodus
9-780-805-490-695 Leviticus, Numbers
9-780-805-490-275 Deuteronomy
9-780-805-490-589 Joshua, Judges
9-780-805-490-572 Ruth, Esther
9-780-805-490-633 1 & 2 Samuel
9-780-805-490-077 1 & 2 Kings
9-780-805-490-649 1 & 2 Chronicles
9-780-805-491-944 Ezra, Nehemiah
9-780-805-490-060 Job
9-780-805-493-399 Psalms 1-50

9-780-805-493-405 Psalms 51-100
9-780-805-493-412 Psalms 101-150
9-780-805-490-169 Proverbs
9-780-805-490-596 Ecclesiastes, Song of
    Solomon
9-780-805-491-975 Isaiah
9-780-805-490-701 Jeremiah, Lamentations
9-780-805-490-787 Ezekiel
9-780-805-490-152 Daniel
9-780-805-493-269 Hosea, Obadiah
9-780-805-493-344 Jonah, Zephaniah
9-780-805-490-657 Haggai, Malachi

New Testament

9-781-558-196-889 Matthew
9-780-805-490-718 Mark
9-780-805-490-046 Luke
9-781-558-196-933 John
9-781-558-196-919 Acts
9-780-805-490-053 Romans
9-780-805-493-252 1 Corinthians
9-780-805-493-351 2 Corinthians
9-781-558-196-902 Galatians
9-780-805-493-276 Ephesians

9-781-558-196-896 Philippians, Colossians,
    Philemon
9-780-805-490-008 1 & 2 Thessalonians
9-781-558-196-926 1 & 2 Timothy, Titus
9-780-805-493-368 Hebrews
9-780-805-490-183 James
9-780-805-490-190 1 & 2 Peter & Jude
9-780-805-492-149 1, 2 & 3 John
9-780-805-490-176 Revelation

SHEPHERD'S NOTES CHRISTIAN CLASSICS

9-780-805-493-474 *Mere Christianity*,
    C. S. Lewis
9-780-805-493-535 *The Problem of Pain/*
    A Grief Observed,
    C. S. Lewis
9-780-805-491-999 *The Confessions*,
    Augustine
9-780-805-492-002 *Calvin's Institutes*
9-780-805-493-948 *Miracles*, C. S. Lewis

9-780-805-491-968 *Lectures to My Students*,
    Charles Haddon
    Spurgeon
9-780-805-492-200 *The Writings of Justin*
    Martyr
9-780-805-493-450 *The City of God*,
    Augustine
9-780-805-491-982 *The Cost of Discipleship*,
    Bonhoeffer

SHEPHERD'S NOTES — BIBLE SUMMARY SERIES

9-780-805-493-771 Old Testament
9-780-805-493-788 New Testament

9-780-805-493-849 Life & Teachings of Jesus
9-780-805-493-856 Life & Letters of Paul

SHEPHERD'S NOTES

When you need a guide through the Scriptures

Romans

HOLMAN
REFERENCE

NASHVILLE, TENNESSEE

Shepherd's Notes—*Romans*
© 1998 by B&H Publishing Group
Nashville, Tennessee
All rights reserved
Printed in the United States of America

978-0-8054-9005-3

Dewey Decimal Classification: 227.1
Subject Heading: BIBLE. N.T. ROMANS
Library of Congress Card Catalog Number: 97–37022

Library of Congress Cataloging-in-Publication Data
Romans / Dana Gould, editor
        p. cm. — (Shepherd's notes)
    Includes bibliographical references.
    ISBN 0–8054–9005–1
    1. Bible. N.T. Romans—Commentaries.   I. Gould, Dana. 1951–.   II. Series
BS2665.5.R66 1998
227'.107—dc21

97–37022
CIP

27 28 29 30 31 32   19 18 17 16 15

CONTENTS

FOREWORD

Dear Reader:

Shepherd's Notes are designed to give you a quick, step-by-step overview of every book of the Bible. They are not meant to be substitutes for the biblical text; rather, they are study guides intended to help you explore the wisdom of Scripture in personal or group study and to apply that wisdom successfully in your own life.

Shepherd's Notes guide you through the main themes of each book of the Bible and illuminate fascinating details through appropriate commentary and reference notes. Historical and cultural background information brings the Bible into sharper focus.

Six different icons, used throughout the series, call your attention to historical-cultural information, Old Testament and New Testament references, word pictures, unit summaries, and personal application for everyday life.

Whether you are a novice or a veteran at Bible study, I believe you will find *Shepherd's Notes* a resource that will take you to a new level in your mining and applying the riches of Scripture.

In Him,

David R. Shepherd
Editor-in-Chief

DESIGNED FOR THE BUSY USER

Shepherd's Notes for Romans is designed to provide an easy-to-use tool for getting a quick handle on this Bible book's important features, and for gaining an understanding of its message. Information available in more difficult-to-use reference works has been incorporated into the *Shepherd's Notes* format. This brings you the benefits of many more advanced and expensive works packed into one small volume.

Shepherd's Notes are for laymen, pastors, teachers, small-group leaders and participants, as well as the classroom student. Enrich your personal study or quiet time. Shorten your class or small-group preparation time as you gain valuable insights into the truths of God's Word that you can pass along to your students or group members.

DESIGNED FOR QUICK ACCESS

Bible students with time constraints will especially appreciate the timesaving features built in the *Shepherd's Notes*. All features are intended to aid a quick and concise encounter with the heart of the message.

Concise Commentary. Short section summaries provide quick "snapshots" of of this pivotal letter.

Outlined Text. A comprehensive outline covers the entire text of Romans. This is a valuable feature for following the narrative's flow, allowing for a quick, easy way to locate a particular passage.

Shepherd's Notes. These summary statements appear at the close of every key section of the narrative. While functioning in part as a quick summary, they also deliver the essence of the message presented in the sections which they cover.

Icons. Various icons in the margin highlight recurring themes in Romans, aiding in selective searching or tracing of those themes.

Sidebars and Charts. These specially selected features provide additional background information to your study or preparation. These include definitions as well as cultural, historical, and biblical insights.

Maps. These are placed at appropriate places in the book to aid your understanding and study of a text or passage.

Questions to Guide Your Study. These thought-provoking questions and discussion starters are designed to encourage interaction with the truth and principles of God's Word.

DESIGNED TO WORK FOR YOU

Personal Study. Using the *Shepherd's Notes* with a passage of Scripture can enlighten your study and take it to a new level. At your fingertips is information that would require searching several volumes to find. In addition, many points of application occur throughout the volume, contributing to personal growth.

Teaching. Outlines frame the text of Romans, providing a logical presentation of the message. Capsule thoughts designated as "Shepherd's Notes" provide summary statements for presenting the essence of key points and events. Personal Application icons point out personal application of Paul's message in Romans, and Historical Context icons indicate where background information is supplied.

Group Study. *Shepherd's Notes* can be an excellent companion volume to use for gaining a quick but accurate understanding of the message of a Bible book. Each group member can benefit by having his or her own copy. The *Note's* format accommodates the study of or the tracing of the themes throughout Romans. Leaders may use its flexible features to prepare for group sessions or use them during group sessions. Questions to guide your study can spark discussion of the key points and truths of Romans.

LIST OF MARGIN ICONS USED IN ROMANS

Shepherd's Notes. Placed at the end of each section, a capsule statement provides the reader with the essence of the message of that section.

Old Testament Reference. Used when the writer refers to Old Testament Scripture passages that are related or have a bearing on the passage's understanding or interpretation.

New Testament Reference. Used when the writer refers to New Testament passages that are related to or have a bearing on the passage's understanding or interpretation.

Historical Background. To indicate historical, cultural, geographical, or biographical information that sheds light on the understanding or interpretation of a passage.

Personal Application. Used when the text provides a personal or universal application of truth.

Word Picture. Indicates that the meaning of a specific word or phrase is illustrated so as to shed light on it.

INTRODUCTION

By every measurement, Paul's letter to the church at Rome is one of the most important ever written. Indeed, from a Christian viewpoint, many would classify it as the greatest letter of all time.

Several considerations support this lofty estimate. For one, Romans has as author one of the most committed of all men, the apostle Paul. No one in the early churches or since has exceeded him in love for Jesus Christ, the Son of God. Furthermore, its message is the grandest of all themes—the grace of God. No New Testament writer experienced that grace more dramatically or proclaimed it more faithfully than Paul.

No wonder, then, that throughout Christian history Romans has played an important role in times of great spiritual renewal. Again and again, God has spoken to men and women at the level of their deepest need through its message.

"Romans in a Nutshell"

Purpose	To express the nature of the gospel, its relation to the Old Testament and Jewish law, and its transforming power.
Major Doctrine	Salvation
Key Passage	Rom. 3:21–26
Other Key Doctrines	God, humanity, and the church
Influence of the Letter	Martin Luther (1515), through preparing lectures on Romans, felt himself "to be reborn."

AUTHOR

The style and language of Romans is consistent with that of Galatians and 1 and 2 Corinthians, the other unquestioned letters of the apostle.

As was the common practice in ancient letter writing, Romans opens with a statement identifying the author. The letter says that it was written by "Paul, a servant of Christ Jesus, called to be an apostle and set apart for the gospel of God" (1:1). It is rarely questioned today that the Paul who wrote the epistle to the Romans was the apostle of that name whose conversion to Christ is recorded in Acts 9 and whose missionary activities dominate the latter half of that book.

AUDIENCE

In the opening chapter, Paul indicated that he was writing his letter to the believers "in Rome" (1:7). What was the makeup of the congregation at Rome? Were they primarily Jewish or Gentile believers? While some passages suggest that Paul's readers were primarily Jewish, other passages seem to require the conclusion that Paul's readers were primarily Gentile converts.

PURPOSE FOR WRITING

Paul wrote Romans with a threefold purpose:

1. He was seeking support for his projected visit to Spain (15:24, 28).
2. He wanted to explain his theology to the Romans and apply it to practical issues in daily life.
3. He wanted to urge the Romans to a greater unity (14:1–15:13).

DATE OF WRITING

Romans was apparently written between A.D. 54 and 58. Evidence indicates that Felix became procurator of Judea in A.D. 59, at which time Paul was in custody in Caesarea (Acts 23:33–27:2). Allowing time for the journey from Corinth to Jerusalem and Paul's subsequent activity before his appearance before Festus, a date somewhere around A.D. 56 is most likely for the composition of Romans.

MAJOR THEMES IN ROMANS

Natural revelation. In Rom. 1:20, Paul set forth two of God's "invisible qualities" that are clearly seen by all—His "eternal power and divine nature." By this Paul meant that the evidence of creation moves a person persuasively toward the conclusion that the Creator is a powerful being and that this power is not limited. Design calls for intelligence, and intelligence speaks of personality. It is God.

The wrath of God. Paul clearly established the responsibility of all people everywhere to acknowledge the existence and basic character of God. There is no excuse for the rebellious who turn from the light of revelation.

A righteousness from God. From the dawn of history, people have struggled to merit acceptance by God. But righteousness cannot be achieved by meritorious activity. Righteousness is a gift from God to those who live by faith

Genesis 15:6 declares that Abraham "believed God," and it was credited to him as righteousness.

Abraham, a man of faith. Abraham was a stalwart patriarch and exemplar of faith and obedience. Since justification depends on faith, Abraham is the father of all who believe, whether Jew or Gentile.

The benefits of believing. In chapters 12–15, Paul clarified the relationship between theology and conduct. He began by pointing out the benefits that accrue to those who believe. These include peace, access, and hope.

Does justification by faith promote sin? The argument of chapter 6 is structured around two basic questions that an opponent of the doctrine of justification by faith would be sure to raise. The questions are intended to point out the unacceptable implications that must follow (from the opponent's point of view) from the idea that a person can be considered righteous on the basis of faith alone. Paul answers emphatically, and the detractors, questions fall by the way.

Life in the Spirit. The Greek word for "spirit" occurs twenty-one times in chapter 8. Paul's concern in this chapter was to show how the Spirit is meant to function in the life of the believer.

To grasp Paul's teaching on the Spirit is to learn the secret of how to live victoriously while surrounded by sin and impaired by human frailty. It is the single most important lesson the Christian can learn.

The triumph of believing. Clearly, living as a Christian in a world dominated and controlled by sin will inevitably involve suffering. Yet we are not alone in our trials. Romans 8:26–30 points out two major sources of help: (1) The intercessory prayer of the Holy Spirit; and (2) the realization that "in all things God works for the good of those who love him."

What about the Jews? Israel's insistence on seeking righteousness by works led to a rejection of all but a remnant. In turning to the Gentiles, God not only fulfilled Old Testament promises but provided the motivation for Israel's return. They will eventually respond in faith and be saved.

Practical Christianity. With chapter 12, Paul shifted his attention to the practical concerns of daily living. The obedience expected is not what we must do to be justified but what we want to do because we are justified.

The obligations of love. In chapter 13 Paul counseled his readers to "put aside the deeds of darkness" (a form of self-love) and "put on the Lord Jesus Christ" (which will issue in genuine love for others). The "obligations of love" will be fulfilled when we identify ourselves with Him so that He who is pure love is allowed to express this love in practical ways.

THEOLOGICAL SIGNIFICANCE OF ROMANS

Paul's message to the Romans means that the church must proclaim that God is the giver of salvation—the gift of righteousness—and this gift is for all who will receive it by faith. The church must not call for a faith that can be separated from faithfulness. Assurance must be grounded not in human decision but in the atoning and justifying work of Jesus Christ.

The believer's righteousness in Christ means that our acceptance and worth before God cannot be earned but only received. When we feel depressed, discouraged, or defeated, we must remind ourselves that God has reconciled us, accepted us, and given us value and significance in His sight because of the atoning work of Jesus Christ.

When troubled from all sides, we are reminded that God is for us, and that nothing can separate us from the love of Christ (8:31–39).

THE MESSAGE OF ROMANS FOR TODAY

Romans lays a solid foundation for an understanding of justification by faith. Faith as an absolute reliance on Jesus Christ, and His work of redemption is clearly presented. Through his arguments and teaching, Paul reveals much about the character and heart of God. From chapter 12 on, Paul dealt with matters of practical Christianity and how life in the Spirit is to be lived out in our daily experience. Paul shows us

When divisions occur in the church, we must turn to Paul's exhortation for mutual love, concern, and service for one another. No one has a superior place in Christ's body because of inherent worth, heritage, accomplishments, or background. There is no place for human boasting or claim of special privilege. All nations are invited to come to Christ, in whom there is no condemnation.

where theology and conduct meet to produce the Spirit-filled life.

QUESTIONS TO GUIDE YOUR STUDY

1. What was Paul's purpose in writing his letter to the Roman believers?
2. Who were Paul's readers? What was the makeup of the congregation at Rome?
3. What key doctrines does Paul emphasize in his letter?
4. Given the various themes covered in Romans, what might we learn from a study of this letter?

Paul's Lists of Spiritual Gifts

Spiritual Gift	Rom. 12:6–8	1 Cor. 12:8–10	1 Cor. 12:28	1 Cor. 12:29–30	Eph. 4:11
Apostle			1	1	1
Prophet	1	5	2	2	2
Teacher	3		3	3	5
Pastor					4
Miracles		4	4	4	
Discernment of Spirits		6			
Word of Wisdom, Knowledge		1			
Evangelists					3
Encouragers		4			
Faith		2			
Healings		3	5	5	
Tongues		7	8	6	
Interpretation		8		7	
Ministry/Serving	2				
Administration			7		
Leaders	6				
Helpers			6		
Mercy	7				
Giving	5				

The Life and Ministry of Paul

MAJOR EVENTS	BIBLICAL RECORDS		POSSIBLE DATES
	Acts	**Galatians**	
Birth			A.D. 1
Conversion	9:1–25	1:11–17	33
First Jerusalem Visit	9:26–30	1:18–20	36
Famine	11:25–30	2:1–10?	46
First Missionary Journey	13:1 to 14:28		47–48
Apostolic council in Jerusalem	15:1–29	2:1–10?	49
Second missionary journey	15:36 to 18:21		
Letter to the Galatians			53–55
Third missionary journey	18:23 to 21:6		53–57
Letters to the Corinthians			55
Arrest and imprisonment in Jerusalem and Caesarea	21:8 to 26:32		57
Imprisonment in Rome	27:1 to 28:30		60–62
Letter to the Ephesians			60–62
Death			67

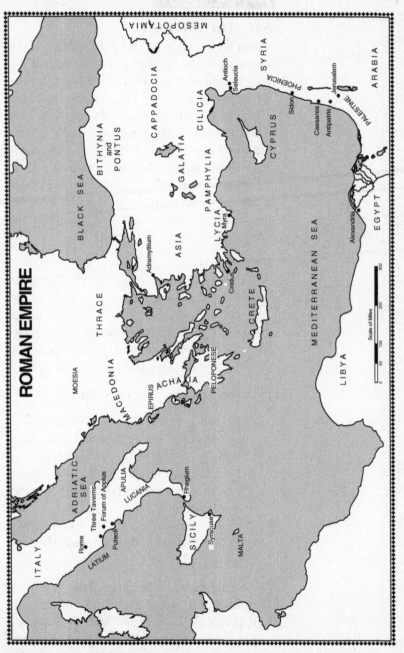

Taken from Robert H. Mounce, *Romans*, vol. 27, New American Commentary
(Nashville, Tenn.: Broadman & Holman Publishers, 1994), p. 20

SALUTATION (1:1–7)

When we write a letter, we put the name of the addressee at the beginning and our own at the end. In Paul's day, people did it differently. The writer placed his name first, the identity of his reader next, and also attached a greeting. Furthermore, in our letters we are content to state the barest details about ourselves and our readers. And our greeting may be more than a "Dear John" or "Dear Friends." The ancient letter writer often expanded the references to himself, his correspondents, and his greetings to enhance his purpose in writing.

Writer (v. 1)

Romans opens with a statement identifying its author. It is rarely questioned today that the Paul who wrote the epistle to the Romans was the apostle of that name whose conversion to Christ is told in Acts 9 and whose missionary activities dominate the latter half of that book.

Paul identified himself in three different ways:

1. He was a *"servant of Jesus Christ."* He belonged without reserve to the one who confronted him on the Damascus road.
2. He was *"called to be an apostle."* God initiated this process. Paul did not choose the role for himself.
3. He had been *"set apart."* He was set apart by God to serve in the interests of the gospel of God.

Paul's Purpose in Writing (vv. 2–6)

To establish his apostolic authority. In verse 1 Paul presented himself as "Paul, a servant of Christ Jesus, called to be an apostle and set apart for the gospel of God." What a remarkable self-introduction! Formerly Paul's zeal for the ancestral tradition had brought him honor and advancement within the ranks of Judaism (Gal. 1:1–14). But now he described himself as Christ's bondslave.

To verify his apostolic message. Paul stated that God had promised His gospel earlier "through his prophets in the holy scriptures." In keeping with other early Christians, Paul saw in the gospel the fulfillment of God's promise in the Old Testament. In verses 3–4 he centered the gospel in Jesus Christ, God's Son. Paul offered two affirmations regarding Jesus: 1) With respect to His fleshly existence or incarnation, He was descended from David. 2) With respect to His present status or exaltation, He was designated "Son of God by his resurrection from the dead: Jesus Christ our Lord."

Readers (v. 7a)

Paul addressed his letter to the Christian believers in the city of Rome. Paul described them as "loved" by God and "called" to be saints.

"Grace and Peace" (v. 7b)

The salutation "grace and peace" combined a Christianized form of the Greek and Hebrew greetings. Real peace comes only as a result of the grace of God. *Grace* is what we receive; *peace* is what we experience as a result of the activities of God on our behalf.

PAUL'S DESIRE TO VISIT ROME (1:8–15)

In keeping with the ancient letter form, Paul continued his opening remarks with expressions of thanksgiving and prayer on his readers' behalf.

The Hellenistic Letter

Generally, Paul's epistles seemed to follow the normal pattern of the Hellenistic letter, the basic form of which consists of five major sections:
1. Opening (sender, addressee, greeting)
2. Thanksgiving or blessing (often with a prayer of intercession, well wishes, or personal greetings)
3. The burden of the letter (including citation of classical sources and arguments)
4. *Parenesis* (ethical instruction, exhortation)
5. Closing (mention of personal plans, mutual friends, benediction).

Several New Testament passages bear witness to the Davidic descent of Jesus (Matt. 1:1; Luke 1:31–33; Acts 2:29–30; Rev. 5:5).

The substance of his prayer is contained in verses 10–15. For a long time Paul had desired to visit Rome, but something had always intervened to prevent a visit. His reasons for wanting to visit believers in the capital city were twofold: (1) he wanted to share some spiritual blessing that would strengthen them; and (2) he wanted to participate in the gospel harvest in Rome, even as elsewhere among the Gentiles.

N

■ *Paul longed to see the believers at Rome.*
■ *Commitment to a common Lord draws the*
■ *people together. To be servants of the same*
■ *master is to be in harmony with one*
■ *another. Paul's special concern was that he*
■ *would be able to share with them some spir-*
■ *itual favor that would provide encourage-*
■ *ment and strength.*

RIGHTEOUSNESS FROM GOD (1:16–17)

These are pivotal verses in the New Testament. They state concisely and with unusual clarity a fundamental tenet of the Christian faith. The heart of verse 16 is that the gospel is the saving power of God.

In his opening remarks, Paul introduced two important features of the gospel and then added a third. We find these features of the gospel described in Romans 1:

1. It is the fulfillment of God's promises (v. 2).

2. It centers in the person of Jesus Christ (vv. 3–4).

3. It is the "power of God for the salvation of everyone who believes" (v. 16).

What is the gospel able to accomplish? The gospel is not simply a display of power but the effective operation of God's power that leads to salvation. It has purpose and direction. The salvation Paul spoke of is more than forgiveness of sin. It included the full scope of deliverance from the results of Adam's sin.

The Power of the Gospel

Aspect of Salvation	Its Work in the Life of the Believer	Sphere of Deliverance
Justification	Being set right with God	Deliverance from the penalty of sin
Sanctification	Growth in holiness	Deliverance from the power of sin
Glorification	Ultimate transformation into the likeness of Christ	Deliverance from the presence of sin

- Verses 16–17 are pivotal verses in the New
- Testament. They state concisely and with
- unusual clarity a fundamental tenet of the
- Christian faith. The gospel is the saving
- power of God.

THE GENTILES (1:18–32)

God's Revelation through Wrath (v. 18)

Paul next pointed to the revelation of God's wrath in His judgment upon sin (v. 18). Romans 1:19–3:20 provides a commentary on this verse.

Paul found his basic concept of justification by faith in Hab. 2:4, "The righteous will live by his faith." The prophet used the term *faith* in the sense of faithfulness or steadfastness. The righteous will be preserved through times of difficulty by their steadfast loyalty to God.

The revelation of God's righteousness in the gospel and the revelation of His wrath are parallel and continuous. That is, God's righteousness is being revealed at all times through the preaching of the gospel of salvation. Also, God's wrath is always being revealed through His abandonment of man to the consequences of his sinful choices (v. 18).

God's Revelation through Nature (vv. 19–20)
The pagan world had an opportunity to know God through His revelation in nature (v. 20). Not only does this verse affirm God's disclosure of Himself in nature, but it also indicates what may be learned about Him—His eternal power and deity—and this knowledge was enough knowledge of God to place men under the responsibility of acknowledging Him and rendering thanks to Him.

We can make three observations about this passage (vv. 19–20):

1. God is the revealer, and nature is the medium of His revelation.
2. God's revelation in nature does not guarantee a positive response.
3. God's revelation of Himself in nature establishes the minimal ground of every person's responsibility before Him.

The age-old question about the salvation of the "heathen" is clearly answered in verse 20. God's revelation of Himself through nature is clear enough to leave all people without excuse for their rebellion against Him.

■ *Paul pointed to the revelation of God's wrath*
■ *in His judgment upon sin and God's disclo-*

- sure of Himself in nature. God's wrath is
- revealed through His abandonment of people
- to the consequences of their sinful choices.
- God's revelation of Himself in nature estab-
- lishes the minimal ground of every person's
- responsibility before Him.

PAGAN RESPONSE (1:21–23, 25)

Rebellion (vv. 21, 25, 28)

Individuals may respond to God's revelation in two ways: in faith or by rejection. They have the capacity to say yes or no to God and to make it stick. "No" is the answer of rebellion, whereas faith is the response of trust and commitment. Self-deification lies at the heart of all human rebellion.

Arrogance (vv. 21–22)

In rejecting the knowledge of God available in creation, people claim to be wiser than God. When a person refuses to accept God as Sovereign, that person is doomed to have less than God as his or her god.

Idolatry (vv. 23, 25)

Just rebellion is an improper attitude toward God, and arrogance is an improper attitude toward self, so idolatry reveals an improper attitude toward creation. A person's refusal to acknowledge God as Sovereign Lord makes idolatry inevitable. It leads to a tragic reversal of the primeval order set forth in Genesis 1:26.

GOD'S JUDGMENT (1:24–32)

For Impurity (vv. 24–25)

People are free to receive or reject God's revelation. However, they are not free to do so without consequences. Verse 24 speaks of "the sinful desires of their hearts." Scripture is clear that the human heart is inclined toward evil. Those who

Wrath of God

"Wrath" is from a word which means to "teem, to swell." (A. T. Robertson, *Word Pictures in the New Testament*, vol. 4, 328). Millard Erickson says: "Anger is not something that God chooses to feel. His disapproval of sin is not an arbirarary matter, for his very nature is one of holiness; it automatically rejects sin. He is ...'allergic to sin,' as it were. The second comment is that we must avoid thinking of God's anger as being excessively emotional. It is not as if he is seething with anger, his temper virtually surging out of control. He is capable of exercising patience and long-suffering, and does so."

Millard Erickson, *Christian Theology*, (Grand Rapids: Baker, 1985), 605.

Homosexuality "cannot be understood as an alternative life-style, somehow acceptable to God" but rather as "a sign of one of the forms of God's wrath takes when he allows us free reign to continue in our abuse of creation and in our abuse of one another as creatures"

P. Achtemeier, *Romans* (Atlanta: John Knox, 1985), 41.

"Depraved"

The word *depraved* is a compound word that combines a negative particle (meaning "not") with the word "approved." It was often applied to metals. (W. E. Vine, "Paul" *Vine's Complete Expository Dictionary* [Nashville, Thomas Nelson, 1996], 526–27). In this passage it carries the idea of "not standing the test" or "not passing the test." It is often translated "reprobate." A "depraved" or "reprobate" mind is one that God cannot approve, and it must be rejected by Him.

rejected God were fools and their hearts were darkened. Verse 24 tells us that God gave them over in their sinful desires, which verse 24 indicates is sexual impurity.

For Sexual Perversion (vv. 26–27)

Paul described this sexual impurity as "degrading . . . their bodies with one another." Romans 1:26–27 contains the clearest teaching in the New Testament on homosexuality. This passage makes the following observations about homosexuality.

1. Homosexuality is an abandonment to "shameful lusts" (v. 26).

2. Homosexuality is "unnatural" (v. 26).

3. Homosexuality involves "indecent acts" (v. 27).

4. Homosexuality is sexual perversion, and it results in a serious breakdown for those involved (v. 27).

For Depraved Reason (vv. 28–32)

For the third time in five verses, Paul wrote that when people disregard God's revelation in nature, He gives them over to the normal consequences that follow. In verse 28 Paul declared that God gives them over to a "depraved mind."

Turning from the light of revelation prevents a person from thinking correctly about the issues of life. God's will and His ways with humans are crucial factors in understanding the moral world in which we live. Secular education, which rules out the hand of God in history, is seriously flawed because it attempts to understand the whole world without acknowledging its source. This is an omission with enormous consequences.

Paul proceeded to characterize the lifestyle of the God-rejecting Gentiles by listing twenty-one negative qualities (vv. 29–32) of those abandoned to their own sinful natures.

■ *The revelation of God's wrath is as authentic*
■ *as His revelation of righteousness. People*
■ *cannot reject God and build a society on a*
■ *solid foundation. Every utopia ventured by*
■ *God-rejecting men is doomed to crumble*
■ *under the sheer weight of its moral corrup-*
■ *tion. Abandoned by God, every such under-*
■ *taking is destined to self-destruct.*

QUESTIONS TO GUIDE YOUR STUDY

1. In his salutation, how did Paul identify himself?
2. Describe the wrath of God. How does God's wrath differ from human wrath?
3. Describe the various pagan responses to God. What is God's judgment for each?
4. What is the Bible's position regarding homosexuality?
5. What does it mean for a person to have a "depraved mind"?

ROMANS 2

Chapter 2 begins with "therefore," a term that normally introduces the result of that which immediately precedes. In this case, however, the connection with chapter 1 is not clear. The final section of that chapter established the need for righteousness among Gentiles, but by the time we reach 2:17, it is obvious that Paul is addressing his remarks to Jews.

GOD'S RIGHTEOUS JUDGMENT (2:1–16)

First, the Jews approved of God's judgment upon the pagan world. Unlike the Gentiles described in Rom. 1:32, they did not applaud those who practiced pagan vices. Quite the contrary: they condemned them. In doing so, they revealed a knowledge of God, an awareness of sin, and an acknowledgment of His right to judge sin.

Did not the approval of God's judgment upon pagan wrong prove that the Jews were rightly related to God? It should have. But what if those who approved God's judgment upon others were themselves guilty of the same sins? Were they to suppose that they would escape the judgment of God?

Agreement without Obedience (vv. 1–11)

No! Paul charged that by passing judgment on the Gentiles, the Jews condemned themselves, because they were doing the same things. To expect God to condone in themselves the sins He punishes in others is to invite God's judgment. It is to treat with contempt the great *kindness*, *tolerance*, and *patience* of God.

Those three terms describe a revelation of God that went beyond the disclosure to the Gentiles through nature of His eternal power and deity (v. 4). They suggest the divine qualities shown through centuries of God's gracious dealings with the Jews.

Judgment with or without the Law (vv. 12–16)

Could the Jews expect preferential treatment for having the Law? Or could the Gentiles plead special consideration for not having it? To be

"But prove yourselves doers of the word, and not merely hearers who delude themselves. For if anyone is a hearer of the word and not a doer, he is like a man who looks at his natural face in a mirrow; for once he has looked at himself and gone away, he has immediately forgotten what kind of person he was" (James 1:22–24, NASB).

sure, God's revelation through the Law provided a great advantage. It made known the will of God more completely, making possible a fuller knowledge of Him.

But the greater opportunity for knowing the will of God included a greater responsibility for keeping it. "All who sin apart from the law will also perish apart from the law, and all who sin under the law will be judged by the law" (v. 12).

There was a real sense in which the Gentiles had access to the Law of God—the inner law of conscience. Through the medium of conscience, God inscribed what the Law required on the hearts of the Gentiles. Thus conscience, as well as nature, constituted a medium through which God sought to reveal Himself to the pagan world. In this way, God brought all people, Gentiles and Jews, under the Law of God.

■ *Through the Law of Moses, God revealed*
■ *Himself to the Jews, and through His law*
■ *written on the heart, He revealed Himself to*
■ *the Gentiles. According to the gospel Paul*
■ *preached, God would judge the secrets of*
■ *both Jews and Gentiles by Christ Jesus on the*
■ *last day (v. 16).*

AUTHENTIC JEWISHNESS IS INWARD (2:17–29)

The Advantages of the Jews (vv. 17–20)

Observe the details Paul mentions in his elaboration of the advantages of the Jews and their pride regarding these advantages.

1. *You call yourself a Jew* (v. 17). We find the earliest use of the term *Jew* in the

Old Testament in 2 Kings 16:6. The Jew was proud to be known as a Jew.

2. *You rely on the Law* (v. 17). The verb translated "rely on" is used in the sense of finding rest or support in something. Thus, the Jew leaned on or found support in the Law.

3. *You glory in (brag about) God* (v. 17). No man has a higher privilege than this: to have his or her glory in God. This is the heart of worship.

4. *You know His will* (v. 18). The Law was regarded as the full revelation of the will of God.

5. *You approve what is excellent* (v. 18). They were able to distinguish between right and wrong because they were instructed in the Law.

6. *You are convinced that you are a guide for the blind, a light for those in darkness (vv. 19–20).* These terms express a low opinion of the Gentiles. They reveal both the high esteem in which the Jew held himself and the low regard that he had for the Gentiles.

The Inconsistencies of the Jews (vv. 21–24)

The charge takes the form of five rhetorical questions and a pronouncement. Observe that in each of the questions Paul charged the Jews with a shocking gap between their profession and their practice. Thus, these verses serve to detail the charge made against the Jews in Rom. 2:3:

1. *You who teach others, do you not teach yourself?* (v. 21). One has to know the truth to teach it. Will one venture to teach to others what he does not apply to himself?

2. *You preach against stealing, do you steal?* (v. 21). This is a reference to the eighth commandment.

3. *You say not to commit adultery, do you commit adultery?* (v. 22). This refers to the seventh commandment. One calls to mind here the incident of the woman taken in adultery and brought before Jesus, as recorded in John 7:53–8:11.

4. *You who abhor idols, do you rob temples?* (v. 22). This refers to those who rob temples, or more generally, to those who commit some irreverent act against a holy place.

5. *You who brag about the law, do you dishonor God by breaking the law?* (v. 23). Breaking the Law made the Jews' bragging about it an empty gesture. God wanted no praise of His revelation in the Law if His people refused to obey the Law.

There are many forms of robbery. The prophet Amos denounced the greedy merchants who were eager for religious holidays to pass so they could resume their sale of wheat with dishonest balances (Amos 8:5).

- *The Jews had no better standing in God's*
- *sight, even though they had received God's*
- *special revelation through the Law of Moses.*
- *Although they knew the will of God*
- *expressed in the Law, they had not kept*
- *the Law.*

Obedience to the Requirement of Circumcision (vv. 25–29)

A third feature of Jewish lostness that obscured their alienation from God was their faithful observance of the Law requiring circumcision.

A real circumcision was not that which was merely external and physical. A person was a Jew only if he was one inwardly. The circumcision that counted was a circumcision of the

Although this rite was practiced by others in the ancient world, it had special meaning for the Jews. God had commanded Abraham to circumcise every male as a sign of the covenant between Abraham and God (Gen. 17:10–17).

heart (see Deut. 30:6). Real circumcision was the work of the Spirit. It did not come through the mechanical observance of the written code. Authentic circumcision was the cutting away of the old sinful nature.

S N

■ *One's heritage and adherence to the rituals of*
■ *the Law did not give a Jew a right standing*
■ *before God. Rather, true Jews were those who*
■ *had received the regenerating work of the*
■ *Spirit in their lives.*

QUESTIONS TO GUIDE YOUR STUDY

1. What makes God's judgments righteous? What do His judgments tell us about Him?

2. What advantages did the Jews enjoy? Why did Paul list them?

3. What were the inconsistencies of the Jews? Why did Paul present these?

4. What is significant about a circumcision of the heart? What does it accomplish that observance of the Law cannot?

ROMANS 3

At this point in his letter, Paul stopped to defend his indictment of Jewish lostness against the objections of an imaginary opponent. No doubt, he had actually encountered such questions from Jewish hearers during his missionary preaching.

THE FAITHFULNESS OF GOD (3:1–8)

Question 1: What Advantage Has the Jew? (vv. 1–12)

What Paul had just written about true Jewish identity and real circumcision was shocking to his fellow Jews (2:25–29). No wonder then that Jewish hearers had likely asked him many questions. Paul's answer to this question is "much in every way!" To begin with, Jews were entrusted with "the very words of God." Most likely this was a reference to the whole Old Testament. (Later Paul cited other reasons in Rom. 9:1–5).

Question 2: Does Jewish Unfaithfulness Nullify God's Faithfulness? (vv. 3–4)

In the previous chapter, Paul had spoken of those hardened and impenitent Jews who were storing up wrath for themselves (2:5). He had described those who were proclaiming the Law fervently to the Gentiles but were practicing it in a shoddy manner before them (2:21–24). Obviously, they were being faithless with regard to the covenant. Did the unfaithfulness of some Jews nullify or cancel the faithfulness of God?

Paul's response was emphatic: "Not at all! Let God be true, and every man a liar." He supported his words with a quote from the last part of Ps. 51:4. He referenced this psalm to emphasize God's vindication in judgment.

Question 3: Is Not God Unjust to Impose His Wrath Upon Us? (vv. 5–6)

The imaginary Jewish objector now began to question God's justice. He argued that his wickedness actually serves God by providing a contrasting background for God's righteousness. What a twisted concept of divine service this represented! Paul again replied emphatically, "Certainly not!" If that were so, how could God

"Not at all!"

This is a very emphatic statement, which we find frequently in the New Testament. It expresses a strong negation to a stated proposition or question. Paul used it here verses 4 and 6. It is comprised of two Greek words, "not" and "to be." To convey their force, these two words have been variously translated as "Let it not happen!" "By no means!" "God forbid!" "Far from it!" "May it never be!"

   "Fitzmyer calls this an 'indignant negative' (*Romans*, 327). Murray says that *me genoita* ["not at all!"] indicates 'the recoil of abhorrence' (*Romans*, 1:94, n.1.)"

Robert H. Mounce, *Romans* (NAC), 104.

judge the world? The moral governorship of the universe was at stake in such an absurd charge.

Question 4: Does Not My Falsehood Cause God's Truth to Abound? (vv. 7–8)

Here we see a contrast between the falsehood of the Jew and the truth of God. The Jew suggested that his falsehood caused the truth of God to abound to His glory. This caused him to wonder why he was still being condemned as a sinner. This question and the previous one amounted to an evangelistic appeal that said, "Let us do evil that good may result" (v. 8) Paul retorted, "Their condemnation is deserved."

God does not need our evil as a *contrast* to His goodness. Rather, He wants our goodness as a *reflection* of His likeness. It praises His glory when God is permitted to create His righteousness in us.

■ *To suggest that God is unfair, as the ques-*
■ *tions of verses 3, 5, and 7 appear to do, is to*
■ *blaspheme God. Those who question God's*
■ *judgment are condemned themselves.*

PAUL'S CONCLUSION: ALL ARE GUILTY BEFORE GOD (3:9–20)

No Fear of God before Their Eyes (vv. 9–18)

"Are we any better?" Paul was once again emphatic—"Not at all!" The Jew was neither better off nor at a disadvantage since it had already been established that both Jew and Gentile are under the condemnation of sin (see 1 Kings 8:46; Gal. 3:22).

To support his charge, Paul strung together several Old Testament passages (vv. 10–18):

Ps. 14:1–3 (vv. 10–12); Ps. 5:9; 140:3 (v. 13); Ps. 10:7 (v. 14); Isa. 59:7–8 (vv. 15–17); and Ps. 36:1 (v. 18). Together they lead up to the ultimate condemnation of verse 18: "There is no fear of God before their eyes." This verse stated the disastrous effects listed in verses 10–17, which were so visible in Paul's day—and in our own.

This entire section (3:9–20) reflects a courtroom scene, which the following chart attempts to capture.

Paul's "Courtroom Scene"

PHASE	VERSE	CONTENT
The Accusation	v. 9	"Jews and Gentiles alike are all under sin."
The Evidence	vv. 10–18	"There is no one righteous, not even one; . . . There is no fear of God before their eyes."
The Courtroom Setting	v. 19	"Every mouth may be silenced and the whole world held accountable to God."
The Verdict	v. 20	"Therefore no one will be declared righteous in his sight by observing the Law; rather, through the Law we became conscious of sin."

The Whole World Is Accountable before God (vv. 19–20)

In bringing his indictment of all men to a close, Paul wrote, "Now we know that whatever the law says to those who are under the law, so that every mouth may be silenced and the whole world held accountable to God." Those under the Law were Jews. Paul focused attention upon them, that they might understand that they, as well as the Gentiles, were

Quoting rather freely from Ps. 143:2, Paul added, "No one will be declared righteous in his sight by observing the law; rather, through the law we become conscious of sin." No human being can be brought into a right standing with God on the basis of doing what the Law requires. Why? Because the Law makes a person conscious of sin. It reveals that we are unable to live up to the righteous requirements of a holy God. The purpose of the Law is to guide conduct, not to provide a method to stand before God on the basis of one's own righteousness.

answerable to God. Both are without excuse before Him (Rom. 1:20; 2:1).

■ *Once again Paul reiterated the theme that*
■ *was so difficult for his Jewish audience to*
■ *understand and accept. No one can be*
■ *brought into a right standing with God on the*
■ *basis of doing what the Law requires. The*
■ *purpose of the Law is to guide conduct, not to*
■ *provide a method to stand before God on the*
■ *basis of one's own righteousness.*

GOD'S WAY OF MAKING US RIGHT WITH HIMSELF (3:21–31)

Apart from the Law (v. 21)

As a devout Pharisee, Paul had believed that he could achieve a right standing with God through keeping the Law. Thus, he was zealous for the traditions of the fathers (Gal. 1:14). He claimed that he was blameless with regard to righteousness under the Law (Phil. 3:6). However, his encounter with the risen Christ on the road to Damascus radically changed all that. No longer would Paul depend upon his obedience to the Law as the basis for his acceptance with God.

When God confronts us in the gospel of Jesus Christ, He does not lay down a new Law for us to keep. We are not invited to attain a right standing with Him through obedience to any religious code. Paul wrote, "But now a righteousness from God, apart from the law." The gospel is nonlegalistic. It is God's good news to a sinful race.

Attested by the Law and Prophets (v. 21)

In Rom. 1:2, Paul indicated that God had promised the gospel beforehand through His prophets in the holy Scriptures. Here he expanded the statement to include the Law as well as the prophets. Through both, God had borne witness to His saving acts in Jesus Christ. The gospel was no innovation. Thus, Paul shared with other early Christians the conviction that the Old Testament pointed forward to the coming of Jesus Christ. The great promises of the Old Testament have their fulfillment in the New.

Experienced through Faith in Jesus Christ (vv. 22–25)

Paul affirmed that God made available to men and women a right relationship to Himself through faith in Jesus Christ. All need to believe in Him, "for all have sinned and fall short of the glory of God." This is the verdict Paul reached regarding the Gentiles, and he repeated it here.

Verses 24–25 are crucial for our understanding of Paul's teaching regarding the death of Jesus Christ on the cross. Here Paul uses three metaphors to describe what God has done for sinful men through Jesus Christ, His Son.

Courtroom. Through the legal metaphor, we see a condemned man in a courtroom as he hears the verdict of acquittal.

Slave. Through the slave metaphor, we see an enslaved man who is redeemed from his bondage and set free.

Ritual Sacrifice. Through the sacrificial metaphor, we see a guilty man from whom the wrath of God has been removed.

27

"Propitiation"

Many have objected to the concept of propitiation which says that God's wrath must be averted if humans are to be justified. John Murray says, "It is one thing to say that the wrathful God is made loving. That would be entirely false. It is another thing to say that the wrathful God is loving. That is profoundly true."

After quoting Murray, Millard Erickson elaborates, "The love which prompted God to send his Son was always there. While the Father's holiness and righteousness and justice required that their be a payment for sin, his love provided it. The propitiation is the fruit of the Father's divine love."

Millard Erickson, *Christian Theology*, 817–818.

All of this is of grace. What God has accomplished through the death of His Son on the cross may be experienced by men through faith.

Shows the Justice of God (vv. 25–26)

God passed over sins previously committed. Does that mean He is indifferent to sin and justice? Paul argued that is not the case. Jesus, God's beloved Son, took on Himself the consequences of sin. Through Jesus' death, God demonstrated at least two truths: (1) That He is a God of justice and (2) that He justifies—or makes right with Himself—those who have faith in Jesus.

The redemptive work of God through His Son Christ Jesus is the most amazing event in the history of the universe. God brought a just sentence of death upon all, for all have sinned. He then provided a sinless sacrifice, His only Son, to atone for the unrighteousness of the wayward human race. What a tragedy when people misinterpret God's forbearance and mercy as indifference toward their sins! (see Eccles. 8:11).

Excludes Pride (vv. 27–28)

What implications does justification by faith have for us at the point of our basic attitude toward God and ourselves? It should make a difference in our lives. Those who imagine they have attained a right standing with God by keeping the Law tend to be proud. But when God's grace is rightly understood, pride becomes an early casualty. Paul declared, "It is excluded." Paul warned the Corinthians, "The person who boasts should boast only of what the Lord has done" (1 Cor. 1:31, NLT).

Affirms God As the God of All Men
(vv. 29–30)

Another important implication of justification by faith is that since God is one, He is the God of all men—Gentiles as well as Jews. This belief was stated by devout Jews every time they recited their traditional confession of faith (the *Shema*), "Hear, O Israel, The LORD our God, the LORD is one. Love the LORD your God with all your heart and with all your soul and with all your strength" (Deut. 6:4).

Upholds the Law (v. 30)

Finally, Paul asked if the principle of faith robs the Law of its rightful role. Does it "nullify" the Law? His answer was, "Not for a moment!" (Moffat). On the contrary, faith puts the Law in its proper place. It plays an essential role in the divine plan, but it was never intended to make it possible for a person to earn righteousness. Faith upholds the Law in the sense that it fulfills all the obligations of the Law.

- *God's justification of those who believe is*
- *provided "freely by His grace." Grace points*
- *to God's free and unmerited favor by which*
- *God has declared believers to have a right*
- *standing in His sight.*

QUESTIONS TO GUIDE YOUR STUDY

1. Why did the Jews think that keeping the Law gave them a right standing before God? What was Paul's response to this belief?

2. Paul declared that all are guilty before God. How was the Jew guilty before God? How was the Gentile guilty before God?

3. How does a person become righteous before God? What does atonement mean?

4. What are two implications of justification by faith that Paul discusses?

The Doctrine of Justification by Faith

Basically, justification is a process by which an individual is brought into an unmerited, right relationship with God. Justification does not encompass the whole salvation process; it does, however, mark that instantaneous point of entry or transformation that makes a person "right with God." Christians are justified in the same way Abraham was—by faith (Rom. 4:16; 5:1). Human works do not achieve or earn acceptance by God. The exercise of faith alone ushers us into an unmerited, right relationship with God (Gal. 2:16; Titus 3:7).

ROMANS 4

Chapter 4 serves as clear proof that the principle of justification by faith apart from works was in fact the principle operative in the Old Testament. It was not some new doctrine created by Paul.

THE BASIS OF ABRAHAM'S RIGHTEOUSNESS (4:1–8)

What was the ground of Abraham's righteousness before God: faith or works? The answer given in Jewish tradition was works. One might wonder how Abraham managed to keep the Law since it was not given until the time of Moses. According to some Jewish tradition, Abraham kept the Law by anticipation.

It follows then that if Abraham were justified by works (or faith regarded as a work of merit), he had ground for boasting. However, Paul appealed to Gen. 15:6 to show that this was not so: "Abraham believed God, and it was credited to him as righteousness." This was a basic biblical teaching about Abraham. God had revealed Himself to Abraham, and Abraham had responded in faith. This faith was reckoned to the patriarch as righteousness. He was justified by faith.

- *Paul offered proof that the principle of justifi-*
- *cation by faith apart from works was in fact*
- *the principle operative in the Old Testament.*
- *Abraham himself was the foremost Old Testa-*
- *ment example (or prototype) of justification*
- *by faith.*

THE MEANING OF CIRCUMCISION (4:9–12)

What about this blessing of a righteousness that is reckoned through faith? Is it for the circumcised only, or does it also include the uncircumcised? Once again, Paul appealed to what the Scriptures taught about Abraham's righteousness. The account of his justification by faith is recorded in Gen. 15:6, and his circumcision is not described until Gen. 17:22–27. This was several years later, when Ishmael was thirteen years old. Thus, at the time that Abraham's faith was reckoned to him for righteousness, he was uncircumcised.

Then what was the meaning of circumcision for Abraham? Paul explained that circumcision was not the work by means of which Abraham attained a right relationship with God. Rather, it was a sign of the justifying faith he already had. Circumcision was a sign of faith, not a substitute for it.

Circumcision and Christianity

Controversy arose in the early church (Acts 10–15) about whether male Gentile converts needed to be circumcised. First-century A.D. Jews disdained the uncircumcised. The leadership of the apostle Paul in the Jerusalem Council was crucial in the settlement of the dispute: Circumcision of the heart by way of repentance and faith were the only requirements (Rom. 4:9–12; Gal. 2:15–21).

- *Paul showed that God declared Abraham*
- *righteous by faith, not by any works or rituals*
- *of the Law.*

God's Promise to Abraham

Abraham's name means "father of a multitude." The first Hebrew patriarch, he became known as the prime example of faith. His name in the beginning was Abram, but this was changed subsequently to Abraham. It was to Abram that God made His covenantal promise in Gen. 17:4–5.

As for me, this is my covenant with you: You will be the father of many nations. No longer will you be called Abram; your name will be Abraham, for I have made you a father of many nations. I will make you very fruitful; I will make nations of you, and kings will come from you. I will establish my covenant between me and you for the generations to come, to be your God and the God of your descendants after you.

Abraham was fully persuaded that God had the power to do what He had promised. Abraham had complete confidence in God's ability and integrity. Faith is total surrender to the ability and willingness of God to carry out His promises.

THE PROMISE OF MANY DESCENDANTS (4:13–25)

God's promises to Abraham and his descendants were not tied to their keeping a law. The promise was of grace—to be believed and received by faith. Putting the relationship between God and humans on a legalistic basis invites the wrath of God. Relationships with a legalistic basis require both parties to carry out perfectly both the spirit and the letter of the Law. Failure to do this results in penalties (wrath) to the offending party. Knowing the weakness of human nature as He does, God knows right relationship must be founded on something other than a legal basis.

Paul climaxed his account of Abraham's justification by faith by reminding his readers that this had meaning for them, too—for "us who believe in him who raised Jesus our Lord from the dead" (v. 24) is also reckoned righteousness. Moreover, Jesus "was delivered over to death for our sins and was raised to life for our justification" (v. 25).

■ *Jesus Christ, crucified and raised to life, is*
■ *God the Father's gracious provision for the*
■ *sins of a fallen race. The simplicity of the*
■ *message makes it clear for all who will hear.*
■ *The power of the message is experienced by*
■ *those who reach out in faith.*

QUESTIONS TO GUIDE YOUR STUDY

1. What was the basis of Abraham's righteousness?
2. What does it mean to be justified by faith?

3. What was the meaning of circumcision for the Jew? Why did Paul declare this ritual unnecessary?

4. What did God promise to Abraham and his descendants?

ROMANS 5

The "therefore" with which chapter 5 begins connects it to what Paul had written in the previous verses. In fact, "since we have been justified through faith" (v. 1) summarizes the entire argument of chapters 1–4.

Those who have placed their trust in Christ can rest assured that their faith has been credited to them as righteousness. Their confidence is based on the fact that Christ was put to death for their sins and raised again that they might be declared just.

THE BENEFITS OF JUSTIFICATION (5:1–11)

A New Relationship with God (vv. 1–2)

Our new relationship with God—based on our being justified by faith—is characterized by peace, access to God, and hope of glory.

Access to God. Through Christ, we have been ushered into the presence of God the Father. By faith we have gained access into this gracious relationship in which we now find ourselves (Eph. 2:18).

Hope of sharing the glory of God. We rejoice in our hope of sharing "the glory of God." Thus, we can face the future with joy. In fact, God's plan that

"Peace with God"

"Peace" is a word rich in meaning. It speaks of the new relationship between God and those who turn to Him in faith. As Paul uses the term here, it does not primarily depict a state of inner tranquillity. It is external and objective. To have "peace with God: means to be in a relationship with God in which all hostility caused by sin has been removed.

we should reflect His glory is now being realized in the lives of obedient believers.

■ *Those justified by faith enjoy a new rela-*
■ *tionship with God. This new standing with*
■ *God is characterized by peace with God,*
■ *access to God, and a joyous hope in sharing*
■ *in God's glory.*

A New Understanding in Suffering (vv. 3–5)

The believers' joy is not something they hope to experience in the future but a present reality even in times of trials and distress. Christian suffering is a source of joy because its purpose is to build character in the believer. Observe the sequence that Paul describes:

The Linked-Chain Process of Christian Suffering

LINK	PRODUCES	RESULT IN THE BELIEVER
Suffering	→	Perseverance
Perseverance	→	Character
Character	→	Hope

"Suffering produces perseverance" (v. 3). The word translated "suffering" literally means "pressure." It describes distress that is brought upon us by outward circumstances.

"Perseverance produces character" (v. 4). The word translated "character" describes the quality of being approved, what has been proved by

---

"Produces"

Each of the three steps above are "produced." The word Paul used is an emphatic form of the word meaning "to work out." It is a word filled with meaning. Because the preposition *down* is often used with a perfective force in composition, a paraphrase might be, "work down to the finish," or "completely produce." (See A. T. Robertson, *A Grammar of the Greek New Testament in the Light of Historical Research*, 606.)

trial. "Endurance brings proof that we have stood the test" (v. 4, NEB).

"Character produces hope" (v. 4). Observe that "hope" is the final level in these three steps toward spiritual maturity. It always burns brightly in those whose character has been developed through overcoming many trials.

Paul maintained that the Christian hope "does not disappoint us." It will never prove to be illusory because "God's love has been poured out into our hearts by the Holy Spirit, whom he has given us."

Hope is not the tuition we pay as we enroll in the school of adversity. Rather, it is the diploma awarded to those who by the grace of God do well on the tests.

■ *Believers have a new understanding of suf-*
■ *fering. Christian suffering is a source of joy*
■ *because its purpose is to build character in*
■ *the believer.*

A New Assurance in Judgment (vv. 6–11)

Another benefit of justification is the assurance it brings about the final judgment. Christian hope is neither wishful thinking nor guesswork. Rather, it is based upon the solid foundation of what God has done for us in the death of His Son.

God took this action on our behalf not because we were good. On the contrary, we were His enemies. We were at our very worst.

Paul's argument is a *how-much-more* argument. If God did this for us when we were at our worst, how much more will He do for us, now that we have been made right with Him by the death of His Son. Looking at the kind and degree of love that God showed us, we have hope and confidence.

The Christian's assurance regarding the final judgment is based on what God has already done (v. 9). Because of it, believers will be saved from the wrath of the last day. God's gracious and decisive action on the believer's part places a solid historical basis under the assurance of final deliverance. That is why Christians "rejoice in God through our Lord Jesus Christ, through whom we have now received reconciliation."

THE GIFT OF RIGHTEOUSNESS (5:12–21)

From Adam to Moses (vv. 12–14)

Beginning at verse 12, we enter Paul's extended contrast between Adam (the first man) and the results of his sin and Jesus Christ (the "second man") and the gracious provisions of His atoning life and death.

But what about those who lived between Adam and Moses? What about the presence of sin before the Law was given? Paul asserted, "For before the law was given, sin was in the world. But sin is not taken into account when there is no law." Adam's sin was expressed as a deliberate transgression of God's commandment. It was not possible for those who lived between Adam and Moses to sin in this way.

Paul explains in verse 14, "Nevertheless, death reigned from the time of Adam to the time of Moses, even over those who did not sin by breaking a command, as did Adam, who was a pattern of the one to come." This verse affirms that humanity headed by Adam was characterized by sin and death even during the time preceding the Law. Also, with reference to Adam as a type of Christ, verse 14 provides a transition to the analogy in the following verses.

Adam and Christ: An Analogy (vv. 15–19)

There are five parallels between Adam and Christ in these verses. The first three are contrasts (vv. 15–17), and the last two are comparisons (vv. 18–19):

1. A contrast between Adam's *trespass*, through which many died, and the *free gift* of God's grace in Christ, which has abounded for many (v. 15).

2. A contrast between the *condemnation* that followed Adam's trespass and the *justification* that follows the free gift of God's grace (v. 16).

3. A contrast between the *death* that reigned through Adam's trespass and the much greater reign in *the lives* of those who receive the free gift of God's grace (v. 17).

4. A comparison between the *condemnation* that came to all people through Adam's trespass and the *acquittal* that comes to all people through Christ's act of righteousness (v. 18).

5. A comparison between the *disobedience* of Adam, through which the many were made sinners, and the *obedience* of Christ, through which the many will be made righteous (v. 19).

The Triumph of Grace (vv. 20–21)

If righteousness is by faith, it is reasonable to ask where the Law fits into the picture. After all, God gave the Israelites an extended code of legislation with the expectation that it would guide their life and conduct. The answer is that the Law was brought in so the offense might increase. Law actually makes wrongdoing all the worse. The Law was never intended to provide salvation but to convince people of their need for it.

"Grace increased"

Where sin increased, grace "superabounded," "surpassed by far," "exceeded immeasurably," "overflowed beyond."

Robert Mounce, *Romans*, NAC, 145.

God lavished His grace upon us beyond all measure. His grace exceeded immeasurably the extent of human sin. God's ultimate purpose in grace is to triumph over the reign of sin and death. What a magnificent portrayal of the achievement of God's justifying work in Christ!

■ *Paul, by way of typology, demonstrated that*
■ *sin and death came to men and women*
■ *through Adam; righteousness and life came*
■ *through Jesus Christ. Sin had been intensi-*
■ *fied by the Law. Thus, greater grace was*
■ *needed. But where sin abounded, grace*
■ *abounded all the more.*

QUESTIONS TO GUIDE YOUR STUDY

1. What characterizes a believer's new relationship with God?
2. What does it mean to have "peace with God"?
3. Describe the three-step process of spiritual maturity through suffering in Rom. 5:3–5. What should be the believer's attitude toward suffering?
4. In what ways does Paul contrast Adam and Christ?

ROMANS 6

Beginning with this chapter, Paul moved ahead to discuss what was to happen in believers' lives after their sins have been forgiven, and they are declared righteous in God's sight. This process of growth in spiritual maturity is the subject of chapters 6–8. This process is called "sanctification," the lifelong process of transformation into the likeness of Christ.

DEAD TO SIN, ALIVE IN CHRIST (6:1–14)

In Rom. 5:20, Paul stated that where sin abounds, God's grace superabounds. What wonderful news this is! It means that no matter how deep the stain of man's sin, the grace of God is greater. Thus, there is hope for all, and men should praise God for His amazing grace.

Yet this great truth about the gospel was liable to grievous distortion by sinful men: "Shall we go on sinning so that grace may increase?" Paul's answer to this rhetorical question is a resounding: "By no means!" How could it be possible for those who have died to sin to continue to live in sin?

Paul describes the Christian's death to sin by reference to baptism. Baptism proclaims with eloquent simplicity what has happened in a person's life.

First, baptism is an identification with Jesus Christ's death, burial, and resurrection. The believer says to the world, "I am with Him. I am His."

Second, baptism is a proclamation that we have died to sin. Our sin and its consequence were borne by Jesus, and our sins were what put Him to death. Realizing the hideous nature of sin, the believer has an aversion to sin.

Third, baptism tells the world that just as God raised Jesus from death—never to die again—so we are being raised from the waters of baptism "to walk in newness of life."

Obviously, the believer doesn't die at baptism in the way Christ died. And he doesn't rise from

William Barclay said, "How dispicable it would be for a son to consider himself free to sin, because he knew that his father would forgive."

Quoted Robert Mounce, *Romans*, NAC, 148.

In many evangelical churches today, people are invited to confess publicly their faith in Christ by walking an aisle and shaking hands with a pastor. But in Paul's day there were no Christian buildings with aisles for people to walk. Instead they made public their confession of faith in Christ by submitting to baptism. It is unlikely that Paul ever faced a situation in which one professed Christian faith and refused to be baptized. Baptism was both the time and the mode of confession whereby one made known his commitment in faith to Jesus Christ as Lord.

death in a resurrected body the way Christ did and the way He will in the future. But baptism conveys to the world a change within the believer that is as radical as Jesus' death and resurrection.

Paul described this radical change in the following way. Prior to conversion, all persons are slaves to sin. In conversion, the old self is crucified with Christ so the body of sin might be done away with. The result is that our slavery to sin is broken.

The believer not only hates sin but has the power to say *no* to it. This is a posture that has to be assumed every day from the time of conversion until the day the believer dies and is fully separated from the presence of sin.

When the believer dies and is in the presence of Christ, he will be incapable of sin. But until then, Paul admonished, "consider yourselves to be dead to sin, but alive to God in Christ Jesus." (Rom. 6:11, NASB). Considering oneself dead to sin doesn't just happen. It's something the believer can and must do—daily.

In verse 13, Paul pointed out that believers have a continuing choice of whether to present the members of their bodies as servants of sin or servants of God. He urged believers to present their bodies to God to serve His good purposes.

"Most commentaries just assume immersion to be the orginial mode (of baptism) as all Christianity did until after the Reformation. Thomas Aquinas and John Calvin conceded this even when they argued for an alternate mode. Luther and Wesley were almost unbending in defense of immersion."

Dale Moody, *Broadman Bible Commentary*, vol. 10, (Nashville: Broadman, 1970), 198.

■ *Salvation as exemplified in baptism so*
■ *changes individuals that they receive a new*
■ *nature which delights in serving God. In con-*
■ *version, Christians pass from an experience*
■ *of slavery to sin to the service of God.*

Paul's Commands in Romans 6:11–13

COMMAND	VERSE	KIND OF COMMAND	EXTENDED MEANING*
"Count your-selves dead to sin."	v. 11	Imperative (do)	"A plea to live up to the ideal of the baptized life."
"Do not let sin reign in your mor-tal body."	v. 12	Prohibition (don't do)	Do not let sin "continue to reign as it once did."
" Do not offer the parts of your body to sin."	v. 13	Prohibition (don't do)	"Stop presenting your members or do not have the habit of doing so."
"Offer yourselves to God."	v. 13	Imperative (do)	"Do it now and completely."
"Offer the parts of your body to him as instruments of righteousness."	v. 13	Imperative (do)	"Do not go on put-ting your members to sin."

* From A.T. Robertson, Word Pictures in the New Testament, vol. 4, "Romans," p. 363.

SLAVES TO RIGHTEOUSNESS (6:15–23)

In Rom. 6:14, Paul declared that Christians are no longer under Law but grace. This verse provides the transition to a restatement of the same problem mentioned in Rom. 6:1: "What shall we say then?" Shall we go on sinning so that grace may increase?" Paul's answer is, "By no means!"

Evidently Paul had encountered Jewish oppo-nents who maintained that law was essential to keep believers from lapsing into pagan sins. Another possibility is that some believers felt

"The walk of grace is the day–by–day issue of the life of grace. Christian ethics are the expression of a relationship with Christ. If a Christian fails morally, it is not because the needed power was not *available*. It is because it was not *appropriated*."

J. W. MacGorman, *Romans*, Layman's Bible Book Commentary, 58.

that since they were under grace instead of law, they could sin without dire consequence. Paul used the analogy of slavery to combat a casual attitude toward sin.

He reminded his readers that, regardless of the religious claims they made, their real master was identified by the commands they obeyed. If they obeyed the commands of sin, then sin was their master and death was their destiny. If they obeyed the commands of righteousness, then righteousness was their master and life was their end.

Verses 20–23 summarize Paul's teaching on the moral consequences of justification by faith. He described two masters, two freedoms, two fruits, and two destinies.

Contrasted Lives

	BELIEVER	NONBELIEVER
Master	Righteousness	Sin
Freedom	Free from sin	Free from righteousness
Fruit	Sanctification	Shameful behavior
Destiny	Eternal life	Death

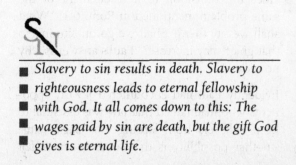

■ *Slavery to sin results in death. Slavery to*
■ *righteousness leads to eternal fellowship*
■ *with God. It all comes down to this: The*
■ *wages paid by sin are death, but the gift God*
■ *gives is eternal life.*

QUESTIONS TO GUIDE YOUR STUDY

1. What does it mean to be "baptized into Christ"?

2. What is the point of Paul's ethical commands in 6:11–13?

3. Contrast the life of a person who is a slave to sin and a person who is a slave to righteousness. What are the major differences?

4. Describe the doctrine of sanctification. How does it happen? What is its result?

Sanctification

Sanctification is the process of being made holy, which results in a changed lifestyle for the believer. Christ's crucifixion makes possible the moving of the sinner from the profane to the holy (that is, "sanctifies," "makes holy") so that the believer can become a part of the temple where God dwells and is worshiped.

Both Paul and Peter affirmed the work of the Holy Spirit in conversion as a sanctification, a making of the believer holy so he or she can come before God in acceptance. Especially in Paul, *justification* and *sanctification* are closely related concepts.

ROMANS 7

In this chapter, Paul pictured himself as one wanting to live righteously and fulfill the demands of the Law, but still within frustrated by sin. Nowhere else in Paul's letters, and nowhere else in ancient literature, is there such a penetrating description of the human plight as in Rom. 7:1–25.

DEAD TO THE LAW (7:1–6)

Paul taught that Christians have died not only to sin but also to the Law. Thus the Law no longer wields authority over them. Paul laid down the principle that the Law exercises lordship over a person only as long as that person "lives." Death cancels the Law's claim upon that individual.

To illustrate this principle, Paul drew on the covenant of marriage. A married woman is legally bound to her husband as long as he lives. If she lives with another man while her husband is living, she violates the Law and is an adulteress. However, if her husband dies, she is free to marry another man.

43

"I have been crucified with Christ; and it is no longer I who live, but Christ lives in me; and the *life* which I now live in the flesh I live by faith in the Son of God, who loved me, and delivered Himself up for me. I do not nullify the grace of God; for if righteousness *comes* through the Law, then Christ died needlessly." (Gal. 2: 20–21, NASB).

Having established the principle that death rendered the Law inoperative, Paul then applied this analogy to the issue at hand—the relation of the Christian to the Law in verse 4. Admittedly, the analogy is not exact.

The important point is that the marriage relationship had been broken by the death of one of it participants. The death of the believer took place when by faith that person became identified with the crucified Christ. Christ's death to and for sin becomes our death to sin (Gal. 2:19–20). The purpose of this death is that we might belong to another husband—to the one who was raised from the dead. Our Savior becomes our new "husband."

And this, in turn, is in order that we may bear fruit to God. If Paul intended us to carry on the analogy of marriage, "bear[ing] fruit" would refer to offspring. He probably had a more general idea in mind, such as "the new life characterized by the good works God prepared beforehand and in which we are to walk." (F. F. Bruce, *The Letter of Paul to the Romans*, 2d ed., TNTC [Grand Rapids: Eerdmans, 1985], 138).

■ *Formerly we were in bondage to written reg-*
■ *ulations. Law was our old master. But now*
■ *we are set free to serve our new master in a*
■ *new way, in the Spirit. Dead to sin and freed*
■ *to live for righteousness, we now live lives*
■ *that bear fruit for God.*

THE LAW AND SIN (7:7–25)

"Is the Law sin?" is Paul's self-imposed question. His emphatic answer is "certainly not!" Any equation of the Law with sin was a shocking distortion to him. However, Paul saw a relationship between the Law and sin, and in verses 7–11, he sought to explain it.

Paul casts his answer in the form of a personal testimony: "I would not have known what sin was except through the Law. For I would not have known what coveting really is if the Law had not said, 'Do not covet.' But sin, seizing the opportunity afforded by the commandment, produced in me every kind of covetous desire" (vv. 7–8).

It was the Law that brought home to Paul the reality of sin. Law defines sin and makes us aware of it. Apart from Law sin exists but cannot be designated as "sin." There may be dangerous microbes in the air, but unless some instrument detects them, they will go unnoticed. The Law does more than show sin for what it is. It provokes sin. Sin seizes the opportunity and arouses within a person a desire to do evil.

Paul raised a second question, "Did that which is good—that is, the Law—become death to me? By no means!" (v. 13). Sin, not the Law, was the culprit. And Paul affirmed that it was through the Law that he came to realize how exceedingly sinful sin was. Suppose that sin could accomplish its work through sinful means only. That would be bad enough, but a particularly treacherous feature of sin is that it can achieve its evil end through that which is good. It can take something as good as the Law of God and accomplish death through it.

"Seizing the Opportunity"

The word translated "opportunity" here and in verse 11 was used in a military context to designate a base of operations or a starting point from which an attack is launched. "A starting place from which to rush into acts of sin, excuses for doing what they [those who sin] want to do" (A. T. Robertson, *Word Pictures in the New Testament*, vol. 4, 367.)

We find this same word in 2 Cor. 5:12; 11:12, and in Gal. 5:13, where Paul taught that Christian liberty can so easily turn to license. In such a case, a person uses his or her liberty as a springboard for sin. (Robertson, 311).

"Sold as a slave to sin"

This phrase means bought and delivered to sin, as a slave to a master. This same verb was used in Matt. 18:25 to describe a debtor being sold into slavery.

At this point Paul made a dramatic switch from past to present tenses as he continued to explain the relation between the Law and sin: "We know that the law is spiritual; but I am unspiritual, sold as a slave to sin."

A slave cannot act upon his own will. He is bound to obey his master. His noble desires will be overruled and crushed by the one who owns him. Through this analogy of slavery, Paul explained why he was unable to obey the Law. As sin's slave, bought and paid for, he had to do his master's bidding. No matter how much he delighted in God's Law, he was powerless to fulfill it.

In verses 21–25, Paul climaxed the account of the struggle in his life between the Law of God and the law of sin. Both of these laws contended for mastery in him. Paul did not offer a neutral battleground. Instead, he was deeply biased in favor of the Law of God, in which he delighted. It appealed to him, and he aspired to fulfill it (v. 22).

John Calvin observed, "This work of God is not completed on the day when it is begun in us, but gradually increases, and by daily advancement is brought by degrees to its completion."

Quoted in Robert Mounce, *Romans*, NAC, 151

But the law of sin would not permit it. This dreadful alien law waged war against the Law of God in Paul and took him captive (v. 23). As a prisoner, he cried out for deliverance, "What a wretched man I am! Who will rescue me from this body of death?" (v. 24). And in the same breath he provided the triumphant answer: "Thanks be to God—through Jesus Christ our Lord!"

Romans 7 does not provide a complete picture of Paul's spiritual experience. In fact, it serves to prepare the reader for what follows. It sets the stage for the triumph of chapter 8. It probably is true that in the lives of most earnest Christians the two conditions Paul described exist in a sort of cycle. Recognition of our inability to live up to our deepest spiritual longings (chap. 7) leads us to cast ourselves upon God's Spirit for power and victory (chap. 8). Failure to continue in reliance upon the power of the Spirit places us once again in a position inviting defeat.

Sanctification is a gradual process that repeatedly takes the believer through this recurring sequence of failure through dependency upon self to triumph through the indwelling Spirit.

- *Paul pictured himself and all believers as*
- *those who long to live on a higher plane. But*
- *they are constantly dragged to the abyss of*
- *disobedience by the power of sin. Struggle*
- *and conflict are typical of Christian experi-*
- *ence, but defeat and despair are not. Through*
- *the death and resurrection of Christ, God has*
- *provided the power for us to live in the free-*
- *dom of the Spirit.*

QUESTIONS TO GUIDE YOUR STUDY

1. How does one become "dead to the law"? Comment on Paul's marriage metaphor.

2. What is the relationship between Law and sin?

3. What is the "new way of the Spirit"? What is its result?

4. In 7:21–25, Paul described a struggle. What was this struggle? How do you deal with this struggle in your own life?

With chapter 8 we arrive at what may be called the inspirational highlight of the book of Romans. The theme of this chapter is living by the Spirit.

Romans 8 is not mere theology. As Paul wrote, his pen gave evidence that he was caught up in an experience of profound worship and spiritual adoration.

DELIVERANCE FROM THE BONDAGE OF SIN (8:1–11)

The new life of the Spirit, made possible through faith in Jesus Christ as Lord, brings deliverance from the old bondage to sin and death. Paul launched this portion of his letter with a mighty declaration of freedom: "Therefore, there is now no condemnation for those who are in Christ Jesus, because through Christ Jesus the law of the Spirit of life set me free from the law of sin and death."

Note the two laws mentioned in this passage: (1) the law of the Spirit of Christ, and (2) the law of sin and death (vv. 1–2).

The law of sin and death. Paul described its work in Rom. 7:14–25. It always lies close at hand, ready to challenge our every desire to do right. It wages a relentless warfare until it has made a captive out of the person who tries to fulfill God's Law.

The law of the Spirit. This law breaks the dominion of the old law of sin and death. Through Jesus Christ men are set free.

Verse 3 tells us how this happens. The heart of the gospel of the grace of God is found in this

"Spirit"

Twenty-one times in Romans 8 the Greek word for *Spirit* or *spirit* occurs. At least eighteen and perhaps twenty of these are references to the Holy Spirit. This means that there are more references to the Holy Spirit in the Romans 8 than in any other chapter of Paul's letters (1 Cor. 12 ranks second with twelve). We have in Romans 8 Paul's fullest discussion of the new life of the Spirit.

verse. The doctrines of the Incarnation and the Atonement come into play here.

The Incarnation. God is not an angry Father waiting to have His wrath against us appeased by the sacrificial intervention of a loving Son. Instead, God the Father acts on behalf of sinful man by sending His Son. Paul described the manner of Christ's coming as "in the likeness of sinful man." This is the Incarnation. Jesus Christ, the Son of God, became one of us in our humanity.

The Atonement. Through the sacrificial death of Jesus on the cross, God achieved our deliverance by condemning sin in the flesh. In His death on the cross, Christ bore the full fury of sin's devastating power.

Paul reminded his readers in verse 9 that they were not under the control of their sinful nature. To the contrary, their lives were under the direction of the indwelling Spirit of God. Furthermore, the indwelling Spirit is the believer's guarantee of future resurrection (v. 11).

■ *The new life of the Spirit, made possible*
■ *through faith in Jesus Christ as Lord, brings*
■ *deliverance from our old bondage to sin and*
■ *death. Christians, controlled by the Spirit of*
■ *God, can experience life and strength in the*
■ *struggles against sin.*

SONSHIP: AN INTIMATE PERSONAL RELATIONSHIP (8:12–17)

Paul next moved to the theme of sonship. He discussed the *test* of sonship, the *privilege* of sonship, and the *assurance* of sonship.

The Test of Sonship (v. 14)

"Those who are led by the Spirit of God are sons of God" (v. 14). A day-by-day response to the leading of the Spirit indicates the one to whom we belong, because we follow the one to whom we belong. This is a more dependable criterion than our emotional highs and lows. Elation without obedience is a fraud.

"Abba! Father!"

Abba is the Aramaic word for *father*. It is the intimate and endearing term by which the child in a Jewish home addressed his father. This term is found only three times in the New Testament: Gal. 4:6; Mark 14:36; and this passage. In Mark 14:36, Jesus used it as He called upon God in Gethsemane. No term serves better than *Abba* or *Father* to qualify the warm, personal relationship to God that His grace has made possible.

The Privilege of Sonship (v. 15)

Paul contrasted the ideas of slavery and adoption as children. He reminded his readers that in turning to Christ they were not enslaved once again to fear. On the contrary, the spirit they received was the consciousness that they had become adopted sons of God. Because of this, they have the privilege to address God as "Abba! Father!"

Privilege also involves responsibility. Paul reminded his fellow Christians that the assurance of resurrection by the indwelling Spirit placed them under obligation to be led by the Spirit of God and not by their sinful nature.

The Assurance of Sonship (v. 17)

As God's children, we are "co-heirs with Christ, if indeed we share in his sufferings in order that we may also share in his glory." Observe Paul's emphasis here on sharing Christ's sufferings (see also Phil. 1:29; 3:10; Col. 1:24). These are not the adversities that come because of our common humanity, such as illness, bereavement, or the loss of employment during a recession.

Rather, they are the sufferings that come from following Christ.

- *In contrast to the control of sin, believers*
- *have received the Spirit of adoption and can*
- *approach God in an intimate way. The*
- *Christian's current suffering is only a pre-*
- *lude to being glorified together with Him.*

Having mentioned in verse 17 that suffering accompanies membership in the family of God, Paul next laid out three grounds of encouragement: (1) the glory that will be revealed (18–25); (2) the help of the Holy Spirit (vv. 26–27); and (3) the fact that all things work together for good (vv. 28–30).

HOPE OF GOD'S ULTIMATE TRIUMPH (8:18–25)

Paul contrasted the suffering of believers which is characteristic of this present age with the glory that will be theirs in the future. In verses 19–22, Paul described creation's involvement both in man's bondage to sin and in his hope of redemption. Genesis 3:17–19 provides background for this discussion. Paul made three statements about the creation:

1. It eagerly awaits the revelation of the sons of God.

2. It was subjected to futility, not willingly, but by the will of God.

3. It is destined to be set free from enslavement to decay and to share in the glorious liberty of God's children.

"Firstfruits of the Spirit"

Paul used the term *firstfruits* in reference to the gift of the Spirit as a pledge (see 2 Cor. 5:5, where the Spirit is given "as a deposit guaranteeing what is to come"). The Spirit is evidence that at the present time we are the sons of God (Rom. 8:14, 16). He is the "down payment" on the inheritance that will be ours as members of the family of God.

   "The Holy Spirit came on the great Pentecost and his blessings continue as seen in the "gifts" in 1 Cor. 12–14, in the moral and spiritual gifts of Gal. 5:22f. And greater ones are to come, 1 Cor. 15:44ff."

A. T. Robertson, *Word Pictures in the New Testament*, vol. 4, 376.

In verses 23–25 Paul resumed his discussion of the believers' present trials. Like creation, we also groan inwardly as we await the final day. Believers yearn for the full adoption as sons that will take place in the resurrection. And we do so as those who have already received "the first-fruits of the Spirit." This is God's pledge of our complete triumph with Christ at the end. At present, this is a hope that we wait for with patience (vv. 24–25).

- *Hope transforms suffering. Paul pointed to*
- *creation's longing for its redemption and*
- *believers' eagerly awaiting their ultimate*
- *adoption and redemption. Here we see God's*
- *plan of redemptive suffering moving to its*
- *fulfillment at the end of the age.*

HELP IN PRAYER THROUGH THE SPIRIT'S INTERCESSION (8:26–27)

Another benefit of the new life of the Spirit is that it is available at a point where we need it most—in our prayers.

Hope carries us through our times of suffering (vv. 24–25). The Spirit also comes to our aid when we find ourselves unable to pray as we ought. Prayer has always been one of the great mysteries of the spiritual life. We understand God is listening, but we sense our inadequacy when we are uncertain about how to pray or for what to pray. For example, how many times have we wondered how to pray for a friend suffering a serious illness?

When our lack of faith undermines certainty in prayer, the Spirit Himself intercedes on our behalf. So intense is the Spirit's prayer that Paul described it as "groans that words cannot express." We may be assured that God understands what the Spirit desires, even though it is inexpressible in human terms. No passage in Scripture provides greater encouragement for prayer.

■ *The Spirit comes to the aid of believers baf-*
■ *fled by the perplexity of prayer and takes*
■ *their concerns to God with an intensity far*
■ *greater than we could ever imagine. Our*
■ *groans become His as He intercedes on our*
■ *behalf in accordance with God's will.*

GOD'S OVERRULING CARE (8:28–30)

We come to one of the favorite verses in Romans. How often in times of trial have believers turned to Paul's reassuring words that God has not deserted us, but He is at work in every circumstance of life: "We know that in all things God works for the good of those who love him, who have been called according to his purpose" (v. 28). This is one of the greatest promises in all the Bible.

Notice the phrase that Paul attached to this promise: "Those who love him, and have been called according to his purpose." Not only is God continually at work, but those for whom He works are steadfast in their love for Him.

The good toward which God is working all things together is that every believer be conformed to the image of Christ.

In verse 30 Paul bridged eternity past and future with his majestic summary of God's redemptive purpose.

"Helps"

"The little English verb *helps* [Rom. 8:26] translates a big verb in Greek. It is used elsewhere in the New Testament only when Martha called for Mary to help her prepare a meal (Luke 10:40)."

Dale Moody, *Broadman Bible Commentary*, vol. 10, 220.

God's Redemptive Purpose in Romans 8:30

WORK OF GOD IN REDEMPTION	MEANING
Predestination	God's grace at work before the foundation of the world
Calling	God's grace confronting us
Justification	God's grace making us right with Himself in the midst of history
Glorification	God's grace in the consummation of this age

S N

■ *Believers may gain assurance knowing that*
■ *God is for them. All that happens to them*
■ *rests in the sovereign hand of God, who in all*
■ *things "works for the good of those who*
■ *love him."*

ASSURANCE OF SALVATION (8:31–39)

Predestination, calling, justification, and *glorification*: These great terms encompass the scope of God's redemptive purpose. Having set forth God's redemptive purpose in verse 30, Paul asked, "What, then, shall we say in response to this?" His answer provides the grandest passage on Christian assurance in the Bible. The following assurances form the solid foundation of our confidence:

1. Our assurance is based on the heavy investment that God has already made in our redemption (vv. 31–32).
2. Our assurance is based upon God's acquittal and Christ's continuing intercession for us (vv. 33–34).

3. Our assurance is based upon God's love for us in Christ, which guarantees that nothing will be able to separate us from Him (vv. 35–39).

After enumerating the various calamities that have assailed God's people (vv. 35–36), Paul claimed, "We are more than conquerors through him who loved us." This statement provides the background for one of the greatest affirmations of faith in God:

"For I am convinced that neither death nor life, neither angels nor demons, neither the present nor the future, nor any powers, neither height nor depth, nor anything else in all creation, will be able to separate us from the love of God that is in Christ Jesus our Lord"(vv. 38–39).

"For Paul, it is not fate, the stars, angelic powers, nor heaven or hell that determines the lives of believers; rather, the faithfulness of Jesus does."

Craig S. Keener, *The IVP Bible Background Commentary,* (Downers Grove: InterVarsity Press), 1993, 432.

■ *Believers can expect difficulties in this age;*
■ *yet they can be certain that nothing will be*
■ *able to separate them from the love of God.*
■ *This recognition of present victory and future*
■ *hope because of God's gracious actions in*
■ *Jesus inspired Paul to ecstatic praise and*
■ *worship of God.*

QUESTIONS TO GUIDE YOUR STUDY

1. What great encouragements is the believer promised in chapter 8? How does each encourage you?

2. What does "sonship" mean for the believer? What does it include? What does it require of us?

3. What does Paul mean by the "firstfruits of the Spirit"?

4. What is the basis for our own assurance of salvation?

ROMANS 9

The triumphant conclusion of Romans 8 turned to a minor key as Paul thought about Israel and its rejection of God's Messiah.

Romans 9–11 is best read and reread as a unit. These three chapters begin with a lament but end with a doxology.

PAUL'S LAMENT (9:1–5)

Ultimate Compassion (vv. 1–3)

When Paul thought of his people and their alienation from God, he felt an overwhelming grief. Placing himself under a solemn oath, he disclosed his anguish in their behalf (vv. 1–2).

How deep was Paul's compassion for his people? He stood ready to forfeit his own hope in Christ if only it could benefit them. This is compassion in its ultimate form. Love knows no greater expression than this. Being an apostle to the Gentiles meant no lessening of Paul's concern for the salvation of his fellow Jews.

The Advantages of the Jews (vv. 4–5)

In verses 4–5, Paul listed several advantages of the Jews that made their rejection all the more tragic:

- They were Israelites.
- They were adopted as sons.
- They experienced the glory of God.
- They were covenant partners with God.
- They had God's Law.
- They had the Temple worship service.

A. T. Robertson said the grief Paul felt at the thought of his brethren was *consuming*

A. T. Robertson, *Word Pictures in the New Testament*, vol. 4, 380.

- They had God's promises.

- They were descendants of the patriarchs.

- They were the people through whom the Messiah was given.

Paul's stance regarding Israel was similar to that of Moses when Israel sinned by creating the golden calf. "But now, if Thou wilt, forgive their sin—and if not, please blot me out from Thy book which Thou has written!" (Exod. 32:32, NASB).

Yet with all these advantages of God's special blessings throughout their history, the Jews did not acknowledge Jesus as the Messiah. As a people, they rejected Him.

■ *Paul's heart was heavy with grief, because*
■ *his own people disdained God's deliverance*
■ *through faith in Jesus Christ.*

GOD'S SOVEREIGNTY (9:6–29)

The "Israel" within Israel (vv. 6–13)

Paul insisted that the word of God had not failed, although most of Israel had not believed in Jesus Christ. This was true because God's promises were not intended for all who could boast of racial descent from Abraham. They constituted the "Israel" within Israel.

Sovereignty is the biblical teaching that God is the source of all creation and that all things come from and depend upon Him (Ps. 24:1). Sovereignty means that God is in all and over all.

Ishmael was as much a son of Abraham as was Isaac. Yet no Jew considered the Ishmaelites to be the children of God's promise to Abraham. Instead, the covenant relationship continued through Isaac.

In verses 10–13 Paul described God's choice of Jacob over Esau. Both sons had the same father and mother. Rebekah conceived both by Isaac (v. 10). Furthermore, God chose Jacob, the younger twin, rather than Esau before they were born (v. 11). Thus, the selection could not have been based on their doing of right or wrong.

The Absolute Freedom of God (vv. 14–18)

God's action with respect to Jacob may have seemed unfair. Paul anticipated a possible charge of injustice against God, but he quickly dismissed it (v. 14). He cited God's message to Moses, "I will have mercy on whom I have mercy, and I will have compassion on whom I have compassion" (v. 15). It is not the exercise of man's will or his striving that compels God to withhold His judgment; it is His mercy (v. 16).

The opposite of showing mercy to the sinner is hardening the heart of the sinner. As God's word to Moses was an instance of the former (showing mercy), so His dealings with Pharaoh provided an example of the latter (v. 17). Paul attributed both the bestowal of mercy and the hardening of the sinner's heart to God's sovereign will (v. 18). Grace does not come as something owed: it is a gift. It has to be or it's not grace.

The "Israel" beyond Israel (vv. 19–29)

This is an exceedingly difficult teaching, and Paul felt the necessity of permitting his imaginary opponent to press his argument still further: "Then why does God still blame us? For who resists his will?" (v. 19). To this pertinent question, Paul gave a sharp rebuke (v. 20). He affirmed the right of the potter to fashion vessels of his choosing out of the same lump of clay. This was true whether the vessels were made for exalted or menial use (v. 21).

Against this background, Paul asked the lengthy hypothetical question in verses 22–24. What if God executes judgment on objects of wrath in order to show His glory to those whom He had prepared to be objects of mercy? Paul did not stop at this point to answer this question. But

"Then I went to the potter's house, and there he was, making something on the wheel. But the vessel that he was making of clay was spoiled in the hand of the potter; so he remade it into another vessel, as it pleased the potter to make. Then the word of the Lord came to me saying, 'Can I not, O house of Israel, deal with you as this potter does?' declares the Lord. 'Behold, like the clay in the potter's hand, so are you in my hand, O house of Israel'" (Jer. 18:3–6, NASB).

from the tone of the question and from the context, we would expect Paul to say something like: "God is God. Who is qualified to evaluate His decisions and actions?"

This is in contrast to the Greek understanding of God expressed in Plato's *Euthyphro*. On this view of right and wrong, justice and injustice were ideas separate from God. For that reason, God's actions could be evaluated by reference to these ideas.

In verses 25–26 Paul turned to several Old Testament passages to show (1) that some Gentiles are included in God's redemptive plans, and (2) that only a remnant of believing Jews will be preserved.

Old Testament Confirmation of God's Redemptive Plan

PASSAGE	ACTION	OLD TESTAMENT CONFIRMATION
Rom. 9:25–26	Redemption includes Gentiles.	Hos. 2:23; 1:10
Rom. 9:27–29	Remnant of Israel will be saved.	Isa. 10:22–23; 1:9

■ *Paul described God's sovereign choice of His*
■ *people. Everything that had taken place in*
■ *redemptive history had been due to God's*
■ *faithfulness to the promise He gave Abraham*
■ *and his descendants. He had chosen Israel to*
■ *serve His purposes as Lord over all.*

Note: Romans 9:30–33 is part of Paul's discussion of chapter 10 and should be studied as a unit with chapter 10. These verses are covered in the following chapter.

QUESTIONS TO GUIDE YOUR STUDY

1. How did the alienation of his people, the Jews, affect Paul? What was his attitude toward them?

2. What added to the tragedy of the Jews' rejection of Jesus Christ?

3. What did Paul mean when he declared that God is sovereign?

4. In support of his argument, Paul provided Old Testament confirmation of God's redemptive plan. Why did he do so? How might this confirmation have impacted his Jewish audience?

"Stumbling block"

A stumbling block is anything that causes a person to stumble or fall. Although this term is sometimes used literally in the Bible, it is most often used as a metaphor. It is used of idols, of God's work with faithless people, and of God Himself in relation to His people. The disobedient are warned that Jesus Himself could be a stumbling block (Rom. 9:32–33). The Greek word *skandalon* was used for the "bait stick" in a trap, the part of the trap to which the bait was attached. It was also used symbolically for the trap itself. In Rom. 9:33, it is "a rock that makes them fall." The word came to refer to "temptation to sin" or "to have false faith."

ROMANS 10

We come now to the second part of Paul's discussion on the relationship of the Jews to the gospel of justification by faith. The last three verses of chapter 9 are part of Paul's discussion of chapter 10 and should be studied as a unit with chapter 10.

In the earlier verses of chapter 9, Paul reminded his readers that the Jews could not establish a legitimate claim on God's favor based on their national heritage. Their history demonstrated that God carries out His purposes with a freedom not limited by human notions of what ought to be. Here Paul showed that the Jews themselves were responsible for their rejection.

THE STONE OF STUMBLING (9:30–33)

Paul pointed to another apparent unfairness regarding Israel and then offered an explanation. The Gentiles, who did not pursue righteousness, had attained it by faith, whereas Israel, having pursued righteousness based on the Law, fell short of it (vv. 30–31). Israel did not understand God's way of making people right with Him. They believed they could make themselves right with God by keeping God's Law. This belief kept them from seeing the numerous ways they fell short of keeping the Law.

A good example of the attitude of righteousness by keeping the Law is seen in a parable Jesus told about a Pharisee who prayed, "God, I thank Thee that I am not like other people: swindlers, unjust, adulterers, or even like this tax-gatherer." Jesus said that the man's prayer was to himself. Luke pointed out that Jesus told this parable "to certain ones who trusted in themselves that they were righteous and viewed others with contempt" (Luke 18:9–14, NASB).

■ *Israel's refusal to believe in Jesus Christ was*
■ *the reason for their rejection. He was the*
■ *stumbling block over whom they had tripped*
■ *and fallen. Righteousness comes by faith and*
■ *faith alone.*

THE TWO WAYS OF SEEKING A RIGHT STANDING WITH GOD (10:1–17)

As he had done in Rom. 9:1–5, Paul expressed again his concern for the salvation of his people. He bore witness to the Jews' zeal for God but lamented that it was not enlightened. Ignorant of the right standing with God made possible through faith, they sought to establish their own right standing with God by keeping the Law. They failed to recognize that Christ put an end to the Law as a way of achieving righteousness

Paul knew firsthand this zeal that was not informed by knowledge. Here he described it to the Galatians: "For you have heard of my former manner of life in Judaism, how I used to persecute the church of God beyond measure, and tried to destroy it; and I was advancing in Judaism beyond many of my contemporaries among my countrymen, being more extremely zealous for my ancestral traditions" (Gal. 1:13–14, NASB).

for everyone who believes (Rom. 10:4; 3:21; Gal. 3:19–4:7).

The Law, instead of providing a way to arrive at a right standing with God, came to an end in Christ. "For Christ means the end of the struggle for righteousness-by-the-Law for everyone who believes in him" (Phillips translation).

There was no question that Paul's Jewish brethren were zealous for God, but unfortunately their zeal was not guided by knowledge. They had no valid insight into God's plan for providing righteousness. They failed to recognize God's way of righteousness—that Christ is the end of the Law.

Paul next contrasted the way of righteousness by Law versus righteousness by faith. He quoted Moses as saying that if a person wants to be righteous based on the Law, he will need to live in accord with that Law (Lev. 18:5). Earlier in Romans he had shown this to be an impossibility. The way of righteousness by faith simply recognized and trusted what God had done.

As there is no distinction between Jew and Greek in sinfulness (Rom. 3:22–23), so there is none between them in salvation (Rom. 10:12; 3:29–30). Belief is the key. Belief depends on hearing. If people hear, someone must proclaim the good news. Paul ended this section with a quotation from Joel 2:32, declaring the good news that "everyone who calls on the name of the LORD will be saved."

"End"

An alternate view of Rom. 10:4 claims that Christ is the "end" of the Law in the sense of its *aim* rather than its *termination*. Thus, the Law has meaning and fulfillment in Christ.

The Way of Salvation

Romans 10:9–10 has long served as one of the most helpful portions of Scripture for pointing out the way of salvation: confession that Jesus is Lord and belief in one's heart that God has raised Him from death. This belief is not merely verbal assent but staking one's entire being on this truth.

■ *Nowhere in Scripture is the universal scope*
■ *of salvation presented with greater clarity.*
■ *Although God's redemptive plan was worked*
■ *out in history through one particular race, it*
■ *was meant from the beginning for the benefit*
■ *of all people.*

The final answer from Isaiah 65:2 is poignant, "All day long I have held out my hands to an obstinate people."

A DISOBEDIENT AND CONTRARY PEOPLE (10:18–21)

In this passage, Paul set up a dialogue between someone who was an advocate for Israel. This advocate asked three questions designed to show that Israel was not at fault in their broken relationship with God. To each of these three questions, Paul cited answers from the Old Testament which showed that Israel was without excuse. Israel was responsible for her rejection. She herself had rejected the word of God.

■ *Israel's rejection had nothing to do with lack*
■ *of opportunity or inability to understand. It*
■ *rested solely upon the nation's willful dis-*
■ *obedience. They insisted on personal merit*
■ *based on works as the way to gain God's*
■ *approval. They had been equipped to under-*
■ *stand that God's requirement for righteous-*
■ *ness is faith.*

QUESTIONS TO GUIDE YOUR STUDY

1. Why was Jesus Christ a stumbling block to Israel?

2. Paul described two ways of seeking a right standing before God. What is the

way of salvation? Why does the way of the Law fail?

3. What were the three objections of Paul's imaginary opponent who defends Israel? How did Paul respond to these objections? What is the point of his response to all three?

4. Paul used Isa. 65:2 to illustrate the real explanation for Israel's rejection of the gospel. Who was responsible for Israel's rejection?

"The Remnant"

"The remnant" consists of the righteous people of God who remained after divine judgment. Old Testament accounts of the remnant abound. For example, Noah and his family may be understood as survivors, or a remnant, of a divine judgment in the flood (Gen. 6:5–8; 7:1–23). In the New Testament, Paul quoted (Rom. 9:25–33) from the prophets Hosea and Isaiah to demonstrate that the saving of a remnant from among the Jewish people was still part of the Lord's method of redeeming His people. There would always be a future for anyone among the covenant people who would turn to the Lord for salvation.

ROMANS 11

Paul began this passage with the rhetorical question, "Did God reject His people?" and his emphatic response, "By no means!" He followed his answer with a discussion of the remnant of Israel, the evangelization of the Gentiles and Israel's jealousy because of the success of the Gentile mission, and the eventual turning of Israel to Christ.

THE REMNANT (11:1–10)

Paul followed up his emphatic denial that God had rejected His people by pointing to Himself as a Jew who was brought to right relationship with God. After all, Paul himself was an Israelite. He was a descendant of the great patriarch Abraham and a member of the tribe of Benjamin. Thus, the rejection of Israel was partial rather than total. There was a remnant of Jewish believers, and Paul was one of them. Although Israel had been disobedient and obstinate, she had not been repudiated as a nation.

If God had rejected the entire nation of Israel, then Paul would not have been able to claim a right standing before God. The truth is that God had not rejected those whom He had chosen as His special people.

Paul found evidence for his teaching about the remnant in the experience of Elijah. At a time of national crisis, the prophet had complained to God that he was the only one who had remained faithful. God then told Elijah there were seven thousand men who had not bowed the knee to Baal (see 1 Kings 19:18).

Making his application, Paul affirmed, "So too, at the present time there is a remnant chosen by grace. And if by grace, then it is no longer by works; if it were, grace would no longer be grace" (Rom. 11:5–6).

■ *Paul taught that since a remnant of Israel*
■ *had believed the gospel, it was a clear indica-*
■ *tion that Israel as a whole would yet believe.*

THE SALVATION OF THE GENTILES (11:11–24)

The description of the hardening of unbelieving Israel in the preceding verses drew from Paul a further question: "Did they not stumble so as to fall beyond recovery?" His inquiry was whether Israel's failure to believe had led to their ruin. Had they stumbled irretrievably? Once again, the answer was, "By no means!"

Verses 11–12 reveal the main points of Paul's discussion for the remainder of the chapter:

1. Through the trespass of Israel, salvation has come to the Gentiles.
2. Through the salvation of the Gentiles, Israel will be provoked to jealousy.

"The LORD called your name,
'A green olive tree,
beautiful in fruit and form':
With the noise of a great tumult
He has kindled fire on it,
And its branches are worthless"
(Jer. 11:16, NASB).

3. Through the inclusion of Israel, great blessings will come to all. Not only was the rejection of Israel *partial*; it was also *temporary*.

In verses 17–24, Paul used the allegory of an olive tree to warn the Gentiles against boasting. The olive tree represented true Israel. Unbelieving Jews were the natural branches that had been broken off. Gentiles were the wild olive branches that have been grafted in. Notice the reasons Paul gave to the Gentiles for not boasting over the Jews:

1. They should remember that they are wild olive shoots who have been engrafted (vv. 17–18).
2. They should understand that the natural branches were broken off because of their unbelief, taking heed not to presume on God (vv. 19–22).
3. They should realize that God has the power to graft the natural branches back into the olive tree, provided that they do not persist in their unbelief (vv. 23–24).

N

■ *Although God may have temporarily rejected*
■ *Israel, He has not finally or irrevocably*
■ *rejected them. When Israel rejected God's*
■ *message, the opportunity was given to the*
■ *Gentiles, who were grafted into the tree.*
■ *Gentiles, however, were warned not to be*
■ *proud of their acceptance but humbly to rely*
■ *on God's grace.*

THE SALVATION OF ISRAEL (11:25–36)

Verses 25–26 need to be understood in the larger context of what Paul has been saying about Israel as a nation. Here Paul boldly announced that all

Israel would be saved. This is an amazing declaration regarding Israel's destiny.

What was the basis for such a claim? Paul described it as a "mystery," a special insight into God's saving plan given him by revelation. The content of the disclosure was that a hardening had come upon a part of Israel "until the full number of Gentiles" come to Christ.

Israel's salvation will be on the same basis as all other people—by responding in faith to the forgiveness made possible by the death and resurrection of Jesus Christ.

Much has been written about this "mystery." Interpreters differ widely in their understanding of this difficult passage. The most probable interpretation of the phrase "all Israel" is that it indicates a great turning of Israel to Christ, without specifying the conversion of every individual Jew, just as the "full number of Gentiles" does not mean that every Gentile will be saved. Paul envisioned a great turning to Christ on the part of the Jewish people. Furthermore, he probably expected this to take place during his lifetime.

With this summation of God's gracious ways with men, Paul burst into praise. This doxology, thought by many to have been written by Paul himself, provides an appropriate finale of the doctrinal portion of Romans and an effective transition to Paul's instruction concerning the practical implications of the gospel.

He magnified the depth of God's riches, wisdom, and knowledge. Who but God could have conceived a plan that would turn disobedience into an occasion for mercy, reaching out universally to all who would believe?

"Mystery"

The New Testament uses the word *mystery* about twenty-five times, twenty-one of which occur in Paul's writings. The "mystery" of the New Testament has been described as an "open secret." Matters previously kept secret in God's eternal purposes have now been or are being revealed (Eph. 3:3–5; 1 Cor. 2:7–8). The mystery of the New Testament appears in the historical activity of the person of Jesus Christ. (Col. 2:2; Eph. 1:9); the indwelling Christ is the hope of glory (Col. 1:26–27). The mystery is received spiritually (Eph. 3:4–5) and manifested in the proclamation of the gospel (Eph. 6:19). Part of the mystery involves the disclosure that Gentiles share in the blessings of the gospel. (Eph. 2:11–13).

It is God who has set everything in motion by His creative Word. He is the source, the agent, and the goal of all that is. All things find their origin in Him. Through Him, everything that exists is sustained and directed. All things exist for His glory. Therefore, to Him be praise and glory forever! Amen.

"Mystery"

This mystery of which Paul spoke in this passage was "not in the pagan sense of an esoteric doctrine for the initiated or an unknown secret (2 Thess. 2:7), or like the mystery religions of the time. Rather, this mystery was the revealed will of God now made known to all (1 Cor. 2:1, 7; 4:1) which included Gentiles (Rom. 16:25; Col. 1:26f.; Eph. 3:3f). It was superior to man's wisdom (Col. 2:2; Eph. 3:9; 5:32; 6:19; Matt. 13:11; Mark 4:11).

- Paul boldly announced that all Israel would
- be saved. He described this as a "mystery."
- This mystery meant that a hardening would
- come upon a part of Israel "until the full
- number of Gentiles" had come to Christ.
- Upon this affirmation, Paul burst into praise
- for God's wisdom and knowledge.

QUESTIONS TO GUIDE YOUR STUDY

1. What was the result of God's rejection of Israel?

2. Describe the concept of "the remnant." How did it relate to Israel's rejection?

3. What is the "mystery" Paul spoke of?

4. Paul's doxology praised God for His plan to transform disobedience into an occasion for His mercy. What does this doxology reveal about the mind and attributes of God?

ROMANS 12

Through the first eleven chapters of Romans, we have followed Paul's presentation of the gospel. Now we come to the last major division of the letter (12:1–15:13), where Paul applies the gospel to everyday living. These four chapters provide the pattern of discipleship for believers.

In this chapter, Paul dealt with the call to commitment, spiritual gifts, and personal relationships.

CALL TO COMMITMENT (12:1–2)

The Greatest Sacrifice: Ourselves (v. 1)

Paul used the language of the altar to urge his readers to costly commitment. He encountered them to offer their bodies as a sacrifice to God. This sacrifice was to be a "spiritual act of worship." These three qualities describe the believer's sacrifice:

When we encounter "therefore," we are directed to look at what has gone before and what is coming after and to discern the connection between them.

1. *It is living.* This concept may provide a contrast with the dead bodies of animal sacrifices, or it could denote the new life that the believer possesses in Christ.

2. *It is holy.* The Christian is set apart for and belongs to God.

3. *It is well-pleasing.* Sacrifices offered to God are not enough in themselves. The offerings must be acceptable to Him.

The Greatest Motivation: The Mercies of God (v. 1)

No greater demand can be made of any Christian than to climb upon God's altar as a living sacrifice. The motivation, therefore, must be equal to the demand. Paul appealed to the correct motivation in the words, "In view of God's mercy." If gratitude to God for His mercies does not compel our devotion to Him, nothing will. Paul never degraded the gospel by diluting its call to commitment.

■ *Paul called on his readers to commit them-*
■ *selves as living sacrifices to God. This sacri-*
■ *fice is a spiritual act of worship.*

The Greatest Threat: The Pressure to Conform to This World (v. 2)

Verse 2 tells of two ongoing activities that carry out the intention of the living sacrifice. The first is negative; the second, positive:

As citizens of heaven (Phil. 3:20), we are to "set [our] minds on things above, not on earthly things" (Col. 3:2). Paul reminded the Galatians that the present age is evil (Gal. 1:4). This age cannot and must not serve as a model for Christian living. Its values and goals do not support growth in holiness.

1. *"Do not conform . . . to the pattern of this world."* Believers are no longer to conform themselves to the present age (the word *world* is literally "age"). This present age is opposed to the world to come.

2. *"Be transformed." Transformation* is the outward expression of what springs from within. Rather than allowing the world to squeeze us into its own mold, Paul told his readers to be "transformed by the renewing of your minds." There is a continuing pressure to adopt the customs and behavior of the world in which we live. Although that influence must be rejected, this alone will never create the kind of change God has in mind for His followers. Genuine change comes from within. We must let ourselves be transformed.

The Greatest Discovery: The Will of God (v. 2)

The purpose of transformation by the renewing of our minds is that we may be able to "test and approve what God's will is."

The greatest discovery of all is the will of God. God's will is good, well-pleasing, and complete:

1. It is *good* because it brings about moral and spiritual growth.
2. It is *pleasing to God* because it is an expression of His nature.
3. It is *perfect* (complete) in that no one could possibly improve on what God wants to happen.

"Test"

The word *test* describes gold tested by refining fires (1 Pet. 1:7).

■ *Believers live as men and women of two ages:*
■ *witnessing to the one that is dying and walk-*
■ *ing toward the one that is dawning. But the*
■ *world does not like this, and it imposes*
■ *relentless pressure upon Christians to con-*
■ *form to its dying ways and values. Thus, Paul*
■ *urged the Roman Christians to resist the*
■ *efforts of a sinful age to press them into its*
■ *mold. Instead, believers are to be trans-*
■ *formed by the renewing of their minds so*
■ *they may know what God has in mind for*
■ *them.*

SPIRITUAL GIFTS (12:3–8)

The Nature of the Church: One Body in Christ (vv. 3–5)

Paul was aware of the consequences of pride in believers. So he cautioned the Christians at Rome not to think of themselves more highly than they ought (v. 3), reminded them that they were all members of one body (vv. 4–5), and encouraged them to use their individual gifts for the benefit of the entire church (vv. 6–8).

They were to to think of themselves with "sober judgment."

To each member of the church at Rome, God had given a measure of faith (see 1 Cor. 12:11; Eph. 4:7). Paul reminded them that as the phys-

"Renewing of your mind"

The word *renew* in the Greek text is a compound of two words: "back" or "again," and "new." This compound is translated "to make new" or "renew." To renew the mind is to adjust one's spiritual vision and thinking to the mind of God, which has a transforming effect on one's life.

A renewed mind is concerned with those issues of life that have lasting importance. By nature, our thoughts tend to dwell on the "fleeting present." But that which passes quickly is normally inconsequential. As Paul explained in 2 Cor. 4:18, "What is seen is temporary, but what is unseen is eternal." The renewed mind enables us to discern the will of God. Released from the control of the world around us, we can come to know what God has in mind for us.

"Sober Judgment"

Robert Mounce pointed out that the use of this term suggests how out of touch with reality the Roman Christians were in their opinions of themselves. Since the metaphor suggests intoxication, we might say they were in danger of becoming "egoholics!"

ical body is made up of many members performing various functions, so also in Christ the many members form one body (see 1 Cor. 12:12–31; Eph. 4:25). Unity in diversity is the theme that runs through this section. Thus unity, however, which is spiritual, was possible only because the members were "in Christ," that is, joined by faith as part of the body of Christ.

The Christian faith is essentially a corporate experience. Although each member of the body comes to faith by an individual act of faith, the believing community lives out its Christian experience in fellowship with one another.

The Variety and Use of Spiritual Gifts (vv. 6–8)

Spiritual gifts are abilities or powers which the Spirit of God bestows upon all believers to equip them for service. These gifts are an important part of the gospel of grace. We are *saved* by grace; we *grow* by grace; and we are *endowed* by grace. Salvation, growth, and service—an experience of God's grace from beginning to end.

Paul mentioned seven different gifts and showed how they were to be exercised (see 1 Pet. 4:10).

- Paul reminded his readers that as the physi-
- cal body is made up of many members per-
- forming various functions, so also in Christ
- the many members form one body. The gift
- each believer has received is the result of the
- gracious outpouring of God's blessing on
- the church.

Spiritual Gifts in the Body of Christ

GIFT	HOW TO BE EXERCISED
Prophecy	Communication of revealed truth that builds up believers
Service	Practical service to help others
Teaching	To provide guidance and moral instruction
Giving	Cheerfully contributing to the needs of others
Encouraging	Encouraging, comforting, and exhorting others
Leadership	Service carried out for the benefit of others
Mercy	Helpful activities such as feeding the hungry, caring of the sick and aging

PERSONAL RELATIONSHIPS (12:9–21)

General Instructions (vv. 9–13, 15–16)

Nowhere in Paul's writings do we find a more concise collection of ethical injunctions. In these verses are several exhortations ranging from love of Christians to hospitality for strangers.

Paul called his readers' attention to the absolute primacy of genuine love. Love must be genuine, not a form of role-playing.

We are to "hate what is evil; cling to what is good." One cannot do the second without doing the first. This insight is one that permissiveness never grasps. Brotherly love is to prevail, and we are to honor others above ourselves.

Love has a capacity to identify with others in their joys or sorrows. To identify with persons in sorrow is sometimes easier than to identify with them in their joys, since we never envy the griefs of others. Love seeks harmony in all personal relationships. It associates readily with the

"Sincere"

In verse 9 the word translated "sincere" is literally "without hypocrisy."

lowly. Freedom from conceit helps to make this possible.

Paul exhorted his readers to several actions:

Never be lacking in zeal (v. 11). In whatever believers do, they are to put their whole heart and soul into it.

Keep your spiritual fervor (v. 11). Believers are to be aglow with the Spirit. The life-giving presence of the Holy Spirit radically alters the way a person lives.

Serve the Lord (v. 11). Christians are to serve the Lord. This service is by no means drudgery.

Be joyful in hope (v. 12). Servants of God continually rejoice in their hope. The word Paul used here speaks of confident trust rather than uncertain expectation.

Be patient in affliction (v. 12). This world will present its share of difficulties, but the believer is to be steadfast in times of trouble.

Be faithful in prayer (v. 12). Most Christians confess the difficulty of maintaining a regular and effective prayer life. The reason is not difficult to discern. If Satan can keep us out of touch with God, he knows we won't cause any problems for his evil kingdom.

Share with believers in need (v. 13). The level of poverty and the need for help were relatively high in the early church. It was critical for believers who had plenty to share their abundance with those in need.

Practice hospitality (v. 13). In a day when inns were scarce and not always desirable, it was critical for believers to extend hospitality to Christians (and others) who were traveling.

When Wronged by Others (vv. 14, 17–21)

Paul provided several exhortations for responding to those who have wronged us.

"Bless those who persecute you; bless and do not curse" (v. 14). Paul urged his readers to invoke God's blessing on behalf of those who persecuted them. This expressed the same attitude Jesus had in His Sermon on the Mount.

"Do not repay anyone evil for evil" (v. 17). We are not to repay evil for evil. This reflected Paul's concern about the impressions Christians make upon unbelievers (see 1 Thess. 4:12; 1 Cor. 6:1; 2 Cor. 8:20–21).

"Live at peace with everyone" (v. 18). As far as is possible, we are called to live at peace with everyone. Jesus pronounced a blessing upon the peacemaker (see Matt. 5:9). The author of Hebrews wrote that we are to "make every effort to live in peace with all men" (Heb. 12:14).

"Do not take revenge" (v. 19). We are not to take vengeance into our own hands. Instead, we are to do good to our enemy. By doing that, we "heap coals of fire on his head."

"Heap Coals of Fire"

"The idea of heaping coals on an enemy's head has led to different interpretations. Some have proposed the remote "Egyptian ritual in which a penitent showed his repentance by carrying on his head a dish containing burning charcoals on a layer of ashes (Manson). This may be in the background of Proverbs 24:21–22, but it is more likely that Paul is advocating nonretaliation in the light of the future rebribution of God."

Dale Moody,
Broadman Bible Commentary, vol. 10, 254–55.

The believer's most powerful weapon against evil is good. To respond to evil is not to overcome it but to add to it. Believers are called upon to live victoriously in a hostile world by following the example of Jesus. God will avenge the wicked and reward the righteous.

QUESTIONS TO GUIDE YOUR STUDY

1. Describe the kind of sacrifice Paul urged his readers to make. What characteristics describe it? What actions does true sacrifice involve on the part of the believer?

2. Contrast the world's pressures on the believer to conform with the inward transformation of the believer. How has God's love changed your attitude toward life and toward other people?

3. The gift each believer receives is the result of the gracious outpouring of God's blessing on the church. What is your gift?

4. What exhortations did Paul give regarding personal relationships? What are some ways these can be applied?

ROMANS 13

In this chapter, Paul discussed the divinely sanctioned role of government and the believer's responsibility to those in power. Christians, like everyone else, are to submit to the governing authorities. Allegiance to God does not take away our responsibility to secular authority.

DUTIES TO THE STATE (13:1–7)

In verses 1–7, Paul provided his readers with instructions regarding governing authorities.

Christians Must Submit to Governing Authorities (vv. 1–2)

The authority of the state is grounded in the will of God (v. 1). To resist rulers is to resist what God has appointed and to incur judgment (v. 2). It is important to remember that govern-

"Render to Caesar the things that are Caesar's, and to God the things that are God's" (Mark 12:17, NASB).

ment is God's way of maintaining the public good and directing the affairs of state.

Christians Must Recognize the Function of Governing Authorities (vv. 3–5)

Rulers maintain order in society by rewarding good conduct and punishing wrongdoing (v. 3). In wielding the sword (the power of life and death), rulers are God's servants who execute His wrath upon wrongdoers (v. 4). We are to submit to their authority because of the fear of punishment as well as the demands of conscience (v. 5). Here we have the biblical basis of the use of force by government for the maintenance of law and order.

Christians Must Support Governing Authorities (vv. 6–7)

Christians are obligated to pay taxes to support the governing authorities. They also are to respect and honor governing authorities (v. 7). Paul did not qualify his statements, and this troubles many modern readers. For example, he did not discuss the limits of Christian obedience, the possibility of the moral justification of revolution, or the duties of rulers to their subjects.

■ *The social benefits that come from a properly*
■ *managed state place the Christian under*
■ *obligation to abide by the accepted regula-*
■ *tions. Undergirding all secular law and*
■ *order is the authority of God delegated to*
■ *those who rule.*

"Submit"

The word *submit* in the Greek text of the New Testament is really a compound of two words, "under" and "to arrange." It means "to put to subjection." In Rom. 13:1, the word means "to be in subjection" to governing authorities.

"This word occurs thirty-eight times in the New Testament, most often in the middle voice, meaning 'to subordinate oneself.' It is used of submission to political authorities (Titus 3:1); wives to husbands (Col. 3:18), the younger toward elders (1 Pet. 5:5). Cranfield argues that the predominant thought is not obedience but the conduct that flows naturally from the recognition that the other person as Christ's representative has an infinitely greater claim on one than one has on oneself.

Romans, 2:660–62 quoted in Robert H. Mounce, *Romans*, NAC, 243, n. 62.

THE PRIMACY OF LOVE (13:8–10)

The previous paragraph dealt with the God-invested authority of the state, submission to rulers, the payment of taxes, and respect for those in public office. These three verses describe the Christian's obligation to all people—the obligation to love (v. 8). All the commandments are summed up in the one sentence, "Love your neighbor as yourself." The need to love is supremely important in view of the critical age in which we live. This obligation to love has no limit. Since love does no wrong to a neighbor, it is the fulfilling of the Law (v. 10).

THE END OF THE AGE (13:11–14)

Here Paul wrote from the perspective of the closing period of the present age.

The world lives as though human history is destined to continue forever. The Christian knows that God is in control of people and nations and is directing history to a predetermined end. Since the end is near, we are to rouse ourselves from sleep. Every day brings us closer to that final day when all we have anticipated in Christ will become a reality.

Because the night is nearly over and the day is about to dawn, it is critical that believers rid themselves of the works of darkness (see Eph. 5:11). It is time to clothe ourselves with the weapons of light. Our conduct is to be decent and honorable.

God used these verses in the conversion of young Augustine in a garden in Milan. He heard some children playing and saying repeatedly, "Take and read; take and read." Augustine responded by opening the Scripture to this passage (Rom. 13:11–14). Upon reading these words, Augustine said, "I had no wish to read more and no need to do so. For in an instant, as I came to the end of the sentence, it was as though the light of confidence flooded into my heart and all the darkness of doubt was dispelled"

Confessions, Book 8, xii.

■ *Christian conduct is vitally related to the*
■ *hope of Christ's return and the believer's ulti-*
■ *mate transformation.*

QUESTIONS TO GUIDE YOUR STUDY

1. What was Paul's view of governing authorities?

2. What did Paul teach about the believer's role in submitting to governing authorities?

3. Why did Paul emphasize the primacy of love in Rom. 13:8–9?

4. What truth prompted Paul's exhortation to the believer to "behave decently"?

ROMANS 14

GUIDELINES FOR ISSUES CONFRONTING THE CHURCH (ROM. 14:1–15:13).

THE PROBLEM (14:2, 5, 21)

Throughout this passage, Paul spoke of two groups of believers, whom he designated as the "weak" and the "strong." He mentioned three points at which the two groups held a sharp difference of opinion: (1) the eating of meat (v. 2); (2) the observance of special days (v. 5); and (3) the drinking of wine (v. 21).

It is interesting to observe how Paul approached a resolution to the problem at Rome. Paul's letters were not intended as abstract treatises on matters ethical and theological. Rather, they were pastoral notes addressed to real-life situations in first-century churches. He offered some Christian guidelines designed to achieve unity in an atmosphere of difference. To help the believers at Rome deal with their problem, he laid down three principles that he discussed in Rom. 14:1–15:13.

PRINCIPLE #1: JUDGMENT IS GOD'S RIGHT, NOT MAN'S (14:1–12)

God has welcomed both the "weak" and the "strong." By grace, both are His servants. As servants, neither has the right to pass judgment upon the other. That right belongs to God alone (v. 4). Each should act in the light of his own convictions regarding the religious scruples in question. Both the observer and the nonobserver of the food laws and special days may have an equal desire to honor the Lord (v. 6).

"Weak faith"

Paul used the term *weak* in a figurative sense here. At Rome there were Jewish Christians who were reluctant to give up certain ceremonial aspects of their religious heritage. Therefore, they maintained a literal obedience to the ceremonial part of the Old Testament Law. They were "weak" in the sense that they were uncertain about how faith in Christ affected the status of Old Testament regulations.

"None of us lives to himself alone" (v. 7) often has been understood in the sense of John Donne's statement, "No man is an island." Paul's statement, however, was not a sociological observation regarding the oneness of the human race. What he said is that all believers live out their lives accountable to God. Decisions about such matters as special days and eating meat are not made in isolation but in accordance with the will of God as understood by the individual.

But the "weak" (immature Christian) must stop passing judgment on his brother who does not share his convictions at such points. And the "strong" must stop scorning his brother who clings to them (v. 10). Both need to realize that they will stand before the judgment seat of God to give an account of themselves to Him (vv. 10–12; see 2 Cor. 5:10).

Paul characterized the "weak" by their lingering legalism. They tended to be harsh in their criticism of those in the church who did not share their opinions. The "strong" were convinced that Jesus Christ had put an end to all religious legalism. They rejoiced in their liberty in Christ. But the "strong" may have been tempted to look down upon their less mature brothers. One *flouted*; the other *flaunted*—both were wrong!

■ *The believers at Rome were experiencing dis-*
■ *agreements about the eating of meat, the*
■ *observance of special days, and the drinking*
■ *of wine. Paul taught that harmonious rela-*
■ *tionships are important. Believers should live*
■ *without judging others.*

PRINCIPLE #2: LOVE REQUIRES SELF-LIMITATIONS FOR THE SAKE OF OTHERS (14:13–22)

Here Paul directed his counsel primarily to the mature. They were able to bear the greater responsibility for healing the breach in fellowship. Thus, he urged them never to place a stumbling block or an occasion to sin in the path of a weaker brother in Christ.

The old taboos on certain ceremonial foods were no longer in force. Jesus taught that it is not what goes into the mouth that makes a person unclean but what comes out (Matt. 15:10–11, 16–20). Nevertheless, Paul was concerned with the effect of this new freedom on those Christians who still felt the regulations of Judaism were not obsolete. Although no food was unclean in itself, if someone regarded it as unclean, then for that person it was.

If the mature ignored the influence of their conduct on the immature, Paul declared, they no longer walked in love (v. 15). Love willingly gives up all liberties that might cause a brother or sister to stumble.

God has called us to a life of faith. Trust is the willingness to put all of life before God for His approval. Any doubt about the rightness of an action removes it from the category of what is acceptable. This principle is of special help to the Christian in what is sometimes called the "gray area." If it is gray to you, it is wrong—not in itself but in the eyes of the one who considers it inappropriate.

God's reign is not fulfilled in food and drink laws, but in "righteousness, peace and joy in the Holy Spirit" (v. 17). Therefore, we are to "make every effort to do what leads to peace and to mutual edification" (v. 19). The peace Paul spoke of here is the peace within the family of believers (see Ps. 34:15).

- *Believers should not influence others to vio-*
- *late their consciences. The mature should not*
- *hinder the weak with their freedom. The*
- *weak should avoid restricting those who*
- *have discovered genuine Christian freedom.*
- *Mutual love and respect are the marks of true*
- *disciples.*

QUESTIONS TO GUIDE YOUR STUDY

1. Paul taught that judgment is a right that belongs to God alone. In light of this, what should be our attitude toward other believers who share different convictions?

2. "None of us lives to himself alone" (v. 7). How do we apply this principle to our congregations and fellowships? To the larger body of Christ?

3. What is the obligation of the stronger believer toward the weaker believer? What is the obligation of the weaker believer toward the stronger believer?

4. All believers are to "make every effort to do what leads to peace and to mutual edification." When differences arise, what steps can believers take to ensure peaceful and edifying results within the body of Christ?

The first thirteen verses of chapter 15 continue Paul's discussion of chapter 14. In dealing with the problem among the believers at Rome, Romans 15:1–13 concludes Paul's message to the Roman Christians. Rounding out chapter 15 is a discussion of Paul's future travel plans, and chapter 16 is the conclusion to his letter.

Psalm 69:9 reflects the selfless life of Christ: "The insults of those who insult you fall on me." As Paul applied this verse, Christ became the speaker.

PRINCIPLE # 3: FOLLOW CHRIST'S EXAMPLE OF FORBEARANCE (15:1–13)

Christ's Example of Self-Denial (vv. 1–3)

Paul's concern that weak and strong Christians live in harmony carries into chapter 15. He linked himself with the "strong" in his appeal that they "bear with the failings of the weak." Rather than pleasing themselves, strong believers are to please their neighbors. By seeking our neighbor's good instead of pleasing ourselves, we follow Christ's example of forbearance. The goal is to help them develop into more mature Christians.

The great example of self-denial for the sake of others is, of course, Jesus Christ. If Christ, the Son of God, did not order His life so as to please Himself, how much more should we give up all personal advantage and follow the path of the Suffering Servant.

The Relevance of Scripture (v. 4)

Verse 4 contains a principle of great significance for the believer. Everything that was written in Scripture in days gone by was written for us (see 1 Cor. 10:11; Rom. 4:23–24). Not only did it serve the needs of its own day, but it is still relevant in the modern world. Scripture is relevant because it meets our deepest needs.

It is through the endurance taught in Scripture and the encouragement it brings that we are enabled to live in hope. The difficulties of today are bearable because God in His Word tells us of a better time to come. He mediates His comfort and encouragement by speaking through His Word to the hearts of receptive believers. To separate ourselves from the Scripture is to turn a deaf ear to the voice of a heavenly Father anxious to console.

First Benediction (vv. 5–6)

Paul's wish was that God would grant the church at Rome a spirit of unity. In the benediction of verses 5–6, Paul prayed that his readers would live in harmony with each other and in such accord with Christ that they would be able to glorify God with one voice.

Paul's perspective was that of Jesus Christ, our model for Christian conduct. We are to think as He does and take on His values and priorities. As members of the church draw closer to Christ, they draw closer to other members of the body. The experience of Christian unity produces a symphony of praise to God in which each voice blends with all others to the glory of God.

Accepting One Another (v. 7)

Both the weak and the strong are to accept one another. The word *accept* carries the idea of a genuine and heartfelt acceptance. That is what it means to follow Christ.

Second Benediction (vv. 8–13)

This second benediction brings the main body of Paul's letter to the Romans to a close.

Christ became a servant of the Jews to demonstrate the truthfulness of God (v. 8). He confirmed the promises made to the patriarchs by fulfilling them. Now the Gentiles can glorify God for the mercy He has shown them.

God's redemptive plan was that through His Son, born a Jew as to His human nature, He might reach out in reconciling love to those of every nation. In support of the universal scope of God's redemptive work through Christ His Son, Paul cited four Old Testament Scriptures.

Old Testament Support for God's Redemptive Work through His Son

PASSAGE	EXPLANATION
1. 2 Samuel 22:50 and Ps. 18:49.	David vows to praise God among the Gentiles. Israel was to be the instrument through whom God's redemptive work would extend to the Gentiles.
2. Deut. 32:43.	From Moses' great hymn celebrating God's victory over Pharaoh and his army: "Rejoice, O nations, with his people."
3. Ps. 117:1.	The salvation of the Gentiles was in God's mind from the very first.
4. Isa. 11.	The Messiah will come as a shoot springing up from the stump of David's family line. He will rule the nations, and on Him the Gentiles will "rest their hopes."

■ *Believers are to follow Christ's example of*
■ *self-denial. Such conduct will result in unity*
■ *and the acceptance of one another. Christ's*
■ *acceptance of both Jewish and Gentile believ-*
■ *ers, played out in the universal scope of His*
■ *redemptive work, is to be the measure of their*
■ *acceptance of one another.*

PAUL'S TRAVEL PLANS (15:14–33)

The Goal of Paul's Ministry (vv. 14–21)

In bringing his letter to a close, Paul expressed his confidence in the character and competence of his readers. He admitted boldness in the way he has written to remind them "on some points" (v. 15). But as a minister of Christ to the Gentiles, he was eager that the offering of the Gentiles as a sacrifice to God would be acceptable.

In seeking to win obedience from the Gentiles, Paul had preached the gospel from Jerusalem to Ilyricum, a province bordering the Adriatic Sea. It was his ambition to preach the gospel in pioneer areas that had never heard it.

Plans to Visit Rome (vv. 22–29)

At the beginning of his letter Paul, mentioned his oft-delayed plans to visit Rome (1:10–15). Now at the end he repeated them. Only here he disclosed a further plan not mentioned earlier—the evangelization of Spain. Feeling that his work in the East had drawn to a close, he wanted to visit Rome briefly and then press on to Spain (Rom. 15:22–25). Obviously he had written this letter to gain the support of the Roman church for his mission to the West.

For the present, however, his visit to Rome and points beyond had to be postponed. First, he had to accompany the delegates from the Gentile churches to Jerusalem with the relief offering (vv. 25–28; see also Acts 20:3–6; 24:17). As soon as this mission was completed, Paul would visit Rome while en route to Spain.

Requests for Prayer (vv. 30–33)

Concerned about the trip to Jerusalem, Paul asked his readers to pray: (1) that he would be delivered from unbelievers in Judea (v. 31);

(2) that his ministry on behalf of the poor believers in Jerusalem would be acceptable to them (v. 31); and (3) that God would permit him his anticipated visit to Rome (v. 32).

A study of Acts 21:15–28:31 provides insights regarding God's answer to these prayer requests.

■ *This concluding section contains Paul's*
■ *travel plans and role as a minister to the*
■ *Gentiles. He wanted to go to Rome in order to*
■ *extend the Christian mission westward to*
■ *Spain. He requested prayer from the church*
■ *for his upcoming mission to Jerusalem.*

QUESTIONS TO GUIDE YOUR STUDY

1. Drawing from Paul's words here and in gospel accounts, in what ways did Jesus demonstrate self-denial? As we follow His example, what principles might we draw on?

2. How is Scripture relevant to believers today? What does 1 Cor. 10:11 teach?

3. What were Paul's travel plans for spreading the gospel? What was his driving force?

4. What support does the Old Testament provide about the universal scope of God's redemptive plan? Why was this plan such "news" to the Jewish leaders of Paul's day?

ROMANS 16

This chapter, made up of five separate segments, contains Paul's final words to the believers at Rome. First, the apostle commended Phoebe to the church at Rome. He followed this with a

Letters of Commendation

The letter of commendation or recommendation was the most common form of letter of mediation in secular letters. Commendations of the following people are embedded in several of Paul's letters: Phoebe (Rom. 16:1); Timothy (1 Cor. 4:17; 16:10–11; Phil. 2:19–24); and Epaphroditus (Phil. 2:25–30).

long list of greetings to his friends and helpers living in the capital city, warnings against false teachers, a section of greetings from Paul's companions, and a closing doxology.

COMMENDATION FOR PHOEBE (16:1–2)

Letters of commendation were well known in the ancient world. Phoebe, a deaconess of the church at Cenchreae, may well have been the bearer of this letter to Rome (v. 1). She had been a faithful helper of many in the work of the gospel. Paul wanted the Roman Christians to receive and help her in any way she needed (v. 2).

PERSONAL GREETINGS (16:3–16, 21–23)

Paul named twenty-six people in verses 3–16. Nowhere else in Paul's writings do we find such a lengthy list of personal greetings. Furthermore, Paul revealed an intimate knowledge of their family relationships and Christian service.

Some have argued that Paul could not have known so many in a church he had never visited. However, the many who are named here may have been Paul's friends and converts in other places who had moved to Rome. Since he had never been to Rome, he would have been eager to greet the ones he knew.

In verses 21–23, Paul sent greetings to the Roman believers from his companions. Those named were with Paul when he was writing the letter, likely from Corinth. One of his companions, Timothy, occupied a very special place in Paul's heart and ministry.

■ *Paul closed his letter typically with greetings*
■ *and commendations from various individu-*
■ *als. Included was a commendation for*
■ *Phoebe, a deaconess of the church at Cen-*
■ *chreae, who may have been the bearer of his*
■ *letter to the Roman believers.*

WARNING AGAINST THOSE WHO CREATE DISSENSIONS (16:17–20)

It is impossible to identify these creators of dissension with any particular group. They have been variously identified as Judaizers, antinomians, or charismatic enthusiasts. They opposed the doctrines that had been taught to the Roman believers. They were self-serving and smooth talking (v. 18).

Those who cause divisions are not serving the Lord but are "slaves of their own base desires" (Moffat, v. 18).

These kinds of people were to be noted and avoided by the church. And the alerted believers could rest assured that the God of peace would soon crush Satan under their feet (v. 20; see Gen. 3:15). This would take place at the end of the age, which Paul expected soon. Verse 20 is a benediction.

Among the "seven [things] that are detestable to [the Lord]," the writer of Proverbs listed in the most emphatic position "a man who stirs up dissension among brothers" (Prov. 6:16, 19).

■ *In every group there seem to be those intent on*
■ *causing trouble. False teachers are identified*
■ *by their teaching. The church must accept or*
■ *reject that which claims to be true on the basis*
■ *of its consistency with revealed truth. God's*
■ *Word stands as the only absolute.*

DOXOLOGY (16:25–27)

Paul closed his letter with a magnificent doxology. In the original Greek text, these verses are one long, involved sentence that reads differently than the usual Pauline doxology. In it we find many of the major themes of the letter to the Romans:

- God is the one who is able to establish and strengthen the believer.

- The gospel is not taught by men but was received by direct revelation from Jesus Christ.

- The gospel centers in the life, death, and resurrection of Jesus Christ.

- The gospel is universal in its purpose.

In the coming ages the songs of the redeemed will ring throughout the courts of heaven. Redemption will be complete. The eternal purpose of God will reach its fulfillment. God will be forever praised.

■ *The objective in preaching the gospel to all*
■ *nations is "that all nations might believe and*
■ *obey him." Therefore, "to the only wise God*
■ *be glory forever through Jesus Christ!"*

QUESTIONS TO GUIDE YOUR STUDY

1. Who was Phoebe? What does her position and importance to Paul's mission say about the role of women in the early church?

2. Paul had never been to Rome. How did he know so many believers in the church at Rome?

3. Paul warned against false teachers. What is our basis for putting into check false teaching in the church?

4. Paul's doxology described several characteristics of God. What are they?

The following list is a collection of the source works used for this volume. All are from Broadman & Holman's list of published reference resources. They accommodate the reader's need for more specific information and an expanded treatment of Romans. All of these works will greatly aid in the reader's study, teaching, and presentation of Paul's epistle to the Romans. The accompanying annotations can be helpful in guiding the reader to the proper resources.

Adams, J. McKee, rev. by Joseph A. Callaway, *Biblical Backgrounds*. This work provides valuable information on the physical and geographical settings of the New Testament. Its many color maps and other features add depth and understanding.

Blair, Joe, *Introducing the New Testament*, pp. 123–31. Designed as a core text for New Testament survey courses, this volume helps the reader in understanding the content and principles of the New Testament. Its features include special maps and photos, outlines, and discussion questions.

Cate, Robert L., *A History of the New Testament and Its Times*. An excellent and thorough survey of the birth and growth of the Christian faith in the first-century world.

Holman Bible Dictionary. An exhaustive, alphabetically arranged resource of Bible-related subjects. An excellent tool of definitions and other information on the people, places, things, and events of the Bible.

Holman Bible Handbook, pp. 671–85. A comprehensive treatment that offers outlines, commentary on key themes and sections, and full-color photos, illustrations, charts, and maps. Provides an accent on the broader theological teachings of the Bible.

Lea, Thomas D., *The New Testament: Its Background and Message*, pp. 393–407. An excellent resource for background material—political, cultural, historical, and religious. Provides background information in both broad strokes on nmspecific books, including Romans.

MacGorman, J. W., *Romans, 1 Corinthians* (Layman's Bible Book Commentary), pp. 15–95. A popular-level treatment of Paul's epistle to the Romans. This easy-to-use volume provides a relevant and practical perspective for the reader.

McQuay, Earl P., *Keys to Interpreting the Bible*. This work provides a fine introduction to the study of the Bible that is invaluable for home Bible studies, lay members of a local church, or students.

———, *Learning to Study the Bible*. This study guide presents a helpful procedure that uses the principles basic to effective and thorough Bible study. Using Philippians as a model, the various methods of Bible study are applied. Excellent for home Bible studies, lay members of a local church, and students.

Mounce, Robert H., *Romans* (The New American Commentary), vol. 27. A scholarly treatment of the text of Romans provides emphases on the text itself, background, and theological considerations.

Robertson, A. T., *A Grammar of the Greek New Testament in the Light of Historical Research*. An exhaustive, scholarly work on the underlying language of the New Testament that provides advanced insights into the grammatical, syntactical, and lexical aspects of the New Testament.

Robertson, A. T., *Word Pictures in the New Testament*, "The Epistles of Paul," vol. 4, pp. 323–430. This six-volume series provides insights into the language of the Greek New Testament. Provides word studies and well as grammatical and background insights into the book of Romans.

SHEPHERD'S NOTES

SHEPHERD'S
NOTES